New

Testament

Exegesis

Revised Edition

NEW

TESTAMENT

EXEGESIS

REVISED EDITION

A HANDBOOK FOR STUDENTS AND PASTORS

GORDON D. FEE

Gracewing.

FOWLER
WRIGHT BOOKS

WESTMINSTER/JOHN KNOX PRESS
LOUISVILLE, KENTUCKY

First published in the British Commonwealth in 1993 by Gracewing, Southern Avenue, Leominster HR6 0QF, England

First published in the United States in 1993 by Westminster/John Knox Press, 100 Witherspoon Street, Louisville, Kentucky 40202-1396

Book design by Susan E. Jackson

Published by Westminster/John Knox Press
Louisville, Kentucky

This book is printed on recycled acid-free paper that meets the American National Standards Institute Z39.48 standard. ∞

PRINTED IN THE UNITED STATES OF AMERICA

9 8 7 6 5 4 3 2 1

British Cataloging-in-Publication Data
A catalogue record for this book is available from the British Library.

ISBN 0 85244 237 8

Library of Congress Cataloging-in-Publication Data

Fee, Gordon D.
   New Testament exegesis : a handbook for students and pastors / by Gordon D. Fee. — Rev. ed.
      p.   cm.
   Includes bibliographical references and indexes.
   ISBN 0-664-25442-X (pbk. : alk. paper)
   1. Bible.   N.T.—Hermeneutics—Handbooks, manuals, etc.
I. Title.
BS2331.F44   1993
225.6′01—dc20   92-35926

To
Maudine, Mark, Cherith, Craig, and Brian
who taught me that exegesis
is not an end in itself,
but must always be applied

We have been studying cheerfully and seriously. As far as I was concerned it could have continued in that way, and I had already resigned myself to having my grave here by the Rhine! . . . And now the end has come. So listen to my piece of advice: exegesis, exegesis, and yet more exegesis! Keep to the Word, to the scripture that has been given to us.

KARL BARTH

(On the event of his formal farewell to his students in Bonn, just prior to his expulsion from Germany in 1935. Quoted in Eberhard Busch, *Karl Barth: His Life from Letters and Autobiographical Texts*; Philadelphia: Fortress Press, 1976.)

CONTENTS

Preface

THE WARM WELCOME WITH WHICH the first edition of this book was received was both gratifying and the certain evidence that such a book was needed. Now—a decade later—a revised edition is called for, not because the basic elements or methods of exegesis have changed, but because much else has happened in ten years. Four matters in particular have called for this new edition.

First, I have spent the past six years teaching exegesis in the context of Regent College (Vancouver, B.C.), where the composition of our student body has forced me to rethink how this material can best be adapted for those who work with the English Bible only. Although many of our students are pursuing career church ministries, the majority are not, and our basic exegesis course is designed to cover both OT and NT, for both M.Div. and Diploma students, the majority of whom do not have Greek. I still require all students to learn the Greek alphabet (as suggested in the Preface to the First Edition), so that they may use the better tools, and I also require them to do assignments that force hands-on use of the various primary sources (in translation) noted in Step 8; but I also have made some adjustments for the sake of non-Greek students, both in the ordering of the steps and in bringing them more quickly to the secondary literature, especially commentaries. These adjustments are now reflected in this revised edition.

Second, there has been a staggering amount of new secondary literature produced during the past decade. This new edition, therefore, allows me opportunity to update the resources in Chapter IV. Not only so, but even the items mentioned in the first Preface need to be updated. Thus in addition to the volumes by Marshall and Harrington, the following very important books should be noted (and probably purchased):

> David A. Black and David S. Dockery (eds.), *New Testament Criticism and Interpretation* (Grand Rapids: Zondervan Publishing House, 1991).
>
> Hans Conzelmann and Andreas Lindemann, *Interpreting the New Testament: An Introduction to the Principles and Methods of N.T. Exegesis;* trans. by S. S. Schatzmann from *Arbeitsbuch zum Neuen Testament,* 8th Ger. ed. (Peabody, Mass.: Hendrickson Publishers, 1988).

The latter book, despite its English subtitle, not only deals with "principles and methods" but also offers major sections on backgrounds, content overviews, and the issues regarding the interpretation of Jesus and early Christianity.

At a much more practical level, and therefore especially for the sake of the English Bible users of this book, useful discussions of many of the matters addressed in the present book can be found in:

> F. Furman Kearley, Edward P. Myers, and Timothy D. Hadley (eds.), *Biblical Interpretation, Principles and Practice: Studies in Honor of Jack Pearl Lewis* (Grand Rapids: Baker Book House, 1986).

Third, during the past decade computer-aided research materials have burgeoned. It is hard to know how much of this material properly fits into a "student handbook," but at least some of the more readily available, or otherwise especially useful, items are noted in Chapter IV.

Fourth, when this book first appeared, rhetorical criticism was just beginning to make its presence felt in exegetical materials. Even though the degree to which NT authors make use of these Hellenistic forms has probably been overstated by its practitioners, this area of study opens up new ways of hearing the NT letters and thus potentially offers many helpful insights into their interpretation. Thus, some discussion of rhetorical matters needed to be added (see I.9.3[E]), as well as some additional bibliography for further study.

As with the first edition, I am indebted to several people for their help in making this new edition possible. Here I record my thanks especially to my teaching assistant for 1991–92, James M. Leonard,

whose help with students went far beyond all normal TA expectations, and who also reread the first edition with an especially critical
eye toward its usefulness to students. I am also grateful to Dr. James
M. Scott of Trinity Western University, who graciously made available to me his especially thorough, unpublished bibliography on
"Lexical Resources for Greek, Latin and Christian Literatures," and
who also supplied the necessary bibliography for computer-aided
research tools.

PREFACE
TO THE FIRST EDITION

A FORMER NEW TESTAMENT COLLEAGUE was once asked by a student
how he could learn to do exegesis, intending that his teacher
should suggest a book. My colleague answered, "You will just have
to take a course." That answer is the tacit admission of what all of us
who teach NT know to be true: There simply is no book that serves
either as a textbook or a guide for students to learn the exegetical
process, from the opening of their Bibles to the writing of the paper.
This book hopes to fill that lacuna.

There are, of course, some useful books available for those who
do exegesis. The closest to the kind I have tried to write is by Otto
Kaiser and Werner G. Kümmel, *Exegetical Method: A Student's Handbook*, rev. ed. (Seabury Press, 1981). But these are essays, not student
guides. The book is useful to a degree, but as anyone knows who
has tried to use it as a text, it is much too general for classroom
purposes. A useful handbook by John H. Hayes and Carl R. Hol-
laday has recently appeared: *Biblical Exegesis: A Beginner's Handbook*
(John Knox Press, 1982). It covers both OT and NT in the same
chapters and approaches the task from the perspective of the various critical procedures.

Two other recent books are especially useful to help the student/
pastor to understand the various concerns and methodologies that
go into the exegetical process for the NT: I. Howard Marshall (ed.),
New Testament Interpretation: Essays on Principles and Methods (Wm.
B. Eerdmans Publishing Co., 1977), 406 pp., and Daniel J. Harring-

15

ton, *Interpreting the New Testament: A Practical Guide* (Michael Glazier, 1979), 149 pp. Either of these books would serve as a good companion to the present book, since they elaborate in considerable detail some of the methodological concerns that are treated in a more "how to" fashion here.

My own reasons for writing this book are several. First, in all my own years of training, I was never taught how to do exegesis. Part of the reason for that, of course, is that I never attended seminary. But as an undergraduate Bible major and as a Ph.D. student in NT studies, I was never specifically trained in exegesis. An undergraduate course in hermeneutics was typical of many such courses—a lot of general, and often helpful, information, but not designed to teach the student how to exegete a piece of text in particular. On the other hand, I saw what was passing for exegesis in many seminaries and graduate schools—basically advanced Greek, in which "exegesis" meant to know the meaning of words and determine "what kind of genitive"—and instinct told me that, necessary and useful as such work was, it was *not* exegesis, but only one part of the whole.

So I did what many of my contemporaries had to do, who also were taught "exegesis" as a part of "hermeneutics" or as "advanced Greek"—I learned on my own. Of course I had many teachers: the better commentaries, such as that by Barrett on 1 Corinthians; my colleagues, especially David M. Scholer, now dean of Northern Baptist Seminary, with whom I team-taught the course in Interpreting the New Testament, and to whom I owe so much that has gone into this book. But much I learned simply by sitting with a piece of text and hammering out the questions on my own.

The impetus for writing the book came initially from my colleague Douglas Stuart, whose similar experience with OT exegesis led him to write the prior companion volume to this one (*Old Testament Exegesis*; Westminster Press, 1980). Soon after Professor Stuart's book appeared, I wistfully voiced the desire to James Heaney of The Westminster Press that I would someday like to write the NT companion volume. Dr. Heaney exercised the proper pressure that finally resulted in "someday" becoming a deadline to be met with a manuscript.

Because this is a companion volume to Professor Stuart's book, I have had his always at my side, and I have purposefully tried to follow his outline as much as possible. Some students, who have already used *Old Testament Exegesis* with profit, at times will even find some verbatim repetition. I make no apologies for that; at many points the two disciplines intersect, and the two volumes are intended to be companions. But because OT and NT exegesis are in fact different disciplines, there are also some obvious differences in the format of the two books. The most notable differences are these: (a) I have included a second chapter in which several of the details of the outline given in Chapter I are elaborated. This second chapter is intended to teach students how to use certain key tools and how to wrestle with the basic *components of* exegesis. (b) Chapter IV (comparable to Professor Stuart's Chapter III) on aids and resources has been keyed to two bibliographies already extant. It did not seem necessary to duplicate this material when several such adequate helps are already available.

Students will soon learn that not everyone will do—or teach—exegesis in precisely the same way. This book attempts to take that into account. The steps given here are not hard-and-fast rules; they are guidelines. If another ordering of steps suits you better, or is followed by your own teachers, then by all means adapt to suit your own needs. What I have tried to provide is a guide to all the steps necessary to do good exegesis. To that end I trust it will be useful.

As with *Old Testament Exegesis,* this book assumes that exegesis requires a minimal knowledge of Greek. But it also is written to encourage the use of Greek by those whose knowledge of the language has grown rusty. Those students without knowledge of Greek will be able to use much of the guide, especially Chapter I. But as you will see in Chapter II, many of the crucial things require some working knowledge of the original language. Here we have offered translations of the Greek so that you might benefit as much as possible from this material. In fact, if you take the time to learn well the Greek alphabet, you will be able to use most of the tools discussed in that chapter. It is hoped that this book will encourage you eventually to acquire a knowledge of the language itself.

I would also like to reiterate here the need to have on hand two of the books Professor Stuart mentions in his Introduction:

Frederick W. Danker, *Multipurpose Tools for Bible Study;* 3d ed. (St. Louis: Concordia Publishing House, 1970);
Richard N. Soulen, *Handbook of Biblical Criticism;* 2d ed. (Atlanta: John Knox Press, 1981).

These books will be excellent supplements to the present one, Danker's being a more thorough examination of the tools mentioned in Chapters II and IV, and Soulen's being a mine of definitions and explanations for nearly all the exegetical terms and techniques you will ever run across.

Finally, acknowledgment must be made of others besides Professors Scholer and Stuart who have contributed to this book. I am indebted to Professor Robert A. Guelich of Northern Baptist Seminary for some initial encouragement and especially for some helpful insights in using the Greek synopsis; to my colleague Dr. Rod Whitacre for generous interaction on the whole, and especially for material on the section on grammatical analysis; to my former student and sometime colleague Gerry Camery-Hoggatt for helpful suggestions at every stage, and especially for material on the documentation of secondary sources. My other two NT colleagues, Royce G. Gruenler and J. Ramsey Michaels, also joined in several hours of vigorous discussion of many parts. Special thanks for the expert typing skills of Holly Greening, Corinne Languedoc, and Anne Swetland.

Analytical
Table of Contents

(For Cross-Reference Use)

Chapter II. **Exegesis and the Original Text**

Chapter III. **Short Guide for Sermon Exegesis**

Chapter IV. **Aids and Resources for the Steps in Exegesis**

ABBREVIATIONS

GNB   Good News Bible, 1976

JAF   Joseph A. Fitzmyer, *An Introductory Bibliography for the Study of Scripture*; Subsidia Biblica, 3. Rome: Biblical Institute Press, 1981

KJV   King James Version

MS. (MSS.)   manuscript(s)

NA[26]   Nestle-Aland, *Novum Testamentum Graece*, 26th ed. Stuttgart: Deutsche Bibelstiftung, 1979

NASB   New American Standard Bible, 1971

NEB   The New English Bible, 1970

NIV   New International Version, 1978

NJB   The New Jerusalem Bible, 1987

NRSV   New Revised Standard Version, 1989

NT   New Testament

OT   Old Testament

REB   The Revised English Bible, 1989

RSV   Revised Standard Version, 1973

UBS[3]   *The Greek New Testament*, 3d ed. United Bible Societies, 1975

INTRODUCTION

THE TERM "EXEGESIS" IS USED in this book in a consciously limited sense to refer to the historical investigation into the meaning of the biblical text. Exegesis, therefore, answers the question, What *did* the biblical author *mean*? It has to do both with *what* he said (the content itself) and why he said it at any given point (the literary context). Furthermore, exegesis is primarily concerned with intentionality: What did the author *intend* his original readers to understand?

Historically, the broader term for the science of interpretation, which included exegesis, was hermeneutics. But since hermeneutics has come to focus more on meaning as an existential reality, that is, what these ancient sacred texts mean for us, I have chosen to limit any use of the term to this more restricted sense of "application."

This book is primarily concerned with the exegetical process itself. Thus the *immediate* aim of the biblical student is to understand the biblical text. However, exegesis should not be an end in itself. Exegetical sermons are usually as dry as dust, informative perhaps, but seldom prophetic or inspirational. Therefore, the *ultimate* aim of the biblical student is to apply one's exegetical understanding of the text to the contemporary church and world. Thus this guide also includes some suggestions for moving "from text to sermon."

The process of doing exegesis, and writing an exegesis paper, is determined in part by the reason(s) one comes to a particular text. Basically there are three such reasons:

27

1. A methodical working of one's way through an entire biblical book.

2. An attempt to resolve the difficulties in a well-known *crux*, or problem passage (1 Cor. 7:14; 15:29; etc.).

3. Preparation for next Sunday's sermon, or lesson, or other related pastoral concerns.

Professors and writers of commentaries usually approach the text for the first reason. In the classroom, students are also involved in this process and frequently write their exegesis papers "in the course of things." It is hoped that more and more pastors will also learn to work exegetically through whole books, not only for immediate teaching or preaching purposes but also for creating a deep reservoir of biblical material in order to inform their entire ministry.

Many student exegesis papers are also written for the second reason. It is hoped that what is learned in trying to resolve "problem passages" will carry over to reason 3 (preaching or pastoral concerns), the most common—and urgent—reason ministers approach the biblical text. Because of this, an entire chapter is devoted to learning how to exegete "short form," for sermon preparation. But one cannot learn to do "short form" well who has not first learned well the whole process.

The guidelines in Chapter I are written from the perspective of reason 2 (dealing with problem passages). Also included (in Step 1) are additional helps for those whose approach is reason 1 (working through an entire book).

The first thing one must note of any biblical text is elementary, but it is also the crucial matter, for it determines much of the rest. *What kind of literature are you exegeting?* The NT is composed basically of four types (genres):

1. The *Epistles*, for the most part, are comprised of *paragraphs* of argument or exhortation. Here the exegete must learn, above all else, to trace the flow of the writer's argument in order to understand any single sentence or paragraph.
2. The *Gospels* are comprised of *pericopes*, individual units of narrative or teaching, which are of different kinds, with different formal characteristics, and which have been set in their present contexts by the Evangelists.
3. *Acts* is basically a series of connected shorter *narratives* that form one entire narrative interspersed with *speeches*.

4. The book of *Revelation* is basically a series of carefully constructed *visions*, woven together to form a complete apocalyptic narrative.

Although they have many things in common, each of these genres also has its own peculiar exegetical problems and "rules." Therefore, in Chapter I the guide will be divided into four parts: (A) some initial steps common to all the genres, (B) some special steps peculiar to each of the genres, (C) some further steps common to all, and (D) some concluding remarks about application.

It is assumed that the guide is not necessarily to be read through in a sitting, but that it will be used in conjunction with the actual work of exegesis. Therefore, if you are exegeting a passage from the Epistles, you should follow the first eight steps common to all (I. 1–8), then follow the three steps peculiar to the Epistles in part B (I.9 [E] to 11 [E]), then skip to part C for Steps 12–15 (I.12–15). Do the same for a paper on the Gospels, Acts, or Revelation. It should be noted that at Step 15, "Write the paper," there are again some different guidelines for a passage from the Epistles or the Gospels. Because Chapter I does not "read right through" for any of the genres, the student will probably find it useful to refer regularly to the schematic diagram found at the beginning of that chapter.

Remember as you use this guide that *all the steps do not apply equally to all NT passages.* For example, some passages will have no textual problems at all, while for others the resolution of the textual question will be a major consideration in understanding. For other texts, the crucial matter will be contextual or lexical, or an insight from the historical context. There is no way to be sure of this in advance. What you need to do is to go through *all* the steps; but as you become familiar with a passage it will tend to become clear to you how to assign the relative weight of each step, and its subpoints.

A final word to those who use only the English Bible. First, you need to take heart that you can learn to do exegesis as well as anyone else. Knowing Greek, of course, gives one obvious advantages in several matters of detail. But the person without Greek, who is willing to do a bit of extra work, can enter into the full joys of this discipline. Thus, you must take seriously the need to learn the Greek alphabet; that will give you direct access to most of the better tools, especially when it comes to the study of words.

Second, the English Bible portion of Step 3 is the absolutely essential matter. Here you will learn not only how to become thoroughly acquainted with your passage, but also how to discover what needs to be investigated. This is your entry point into the content questions. The point of this exercise is *not*, I repeat, *not* to make choices between the various translations as to which one you prefer! Rather, it is to lead you to the secondary sources where these matters are discussed. But the goal is to learn the whole method well enough so that even here you can learn to have confidence in making up your own mind.

Third, you will help yourself immensely if you will read widely in the secondary literature for each step listed in Chapter IV. Items that are especially helpful for beginning students in these various disciplines are carefully marked.

In time you may find it possible to learn the language itself, at least at a very basic level. If you do, you will find to your delight that it is not nearly as difficult as you have imagined, or as others have suggested.

I

GUIDE FOR FULL EXEGESIS

Be sure to read the Introduction first!

HE KEY TO GOOD EXEGESIS is the ability to ask the right questions of the text in order to get at the author's intended meaning. Good exegetical questions fall into two basic categories: questions of *content* (what is said) and of *context* (why it is said).

The contextual questions are of two kinds: historical and literary. Historical context has to do both with the general historical setting of a document (e.g., the city of Corinth, its geography, people, religions, economy, etc.) and with the specific occasion of the document (i.e., why it was written). Literary context has to do with why a given thing was said at a given point in the argument or narrative.

The questions of content are basically of four kinds: textual criticism (the determination of the actual wording of the author), lexical data (the meaning of words), grammatical data (the relationship of words to one another), and historical-cultural background (the relationship of words and ideas to the background and culture of the author and his readers).

Good exegesis, therefore, is the happy combination—or careful integration—of all these data into a readable presentation. The aim of such a presentation is not originality or uniqueness, but a clear understanding of the author's original intention. The schematic on the following pages gives you an overview of the process. The rest of the chapter leads you through each of the steps.

WRITING AN EXEGESIS PAPER

A SCHEMATIC

STEP 1:

Survey the historical context in general.

STEP 2:

Confirm the limits of the passage.

STEP 3:

Become thoroughly acquainted with your paragraph/pericope.

STEP 4:

Analyze sentence structures and syntactical relationships. (See II.1)

STEP 5:

Establish the text. (See II.2)

STEP 6:

Analyze the grammar. (See II.3)

STEP 7:

Analyze significant words. (See II.4)

STEP 8:
Research the historical-cultural background. (See II.5)

Go to Steps 9–11 on the basis of the literary genre of your passage.

EPISTLES

STEP 9 (E):

Determine the formal characteristics of the Epistle.

STEP 10 (E):

Examine the historical context in particular.

STEP 11 (E):

Determine the literary context.

GOSPELS

STEP 9 (G):

Determine the formal character of the pericope or saying.

STEP 10 (G):

Analyze the pericope in a Gospel synopsis. (See II.6)

STEP 11 (G):

Consider possible life settings in the ministry of Jesus.

ACTS

Step 10 (A):

Research the historical questions.

Step 11 (A):

Determine the literary context.

Complete the exegesis by going through Steps 12–15.

Step 12:

Consider the broader biblical and theological contexts.

Step 13:

Consult secondary literature.

THE REVELATION

Step 9 (R):

Understand the formal character of the Revelation.

Step 10 (R):

Determine the historical context.

Step 11 (R):

Determine the literary context.

Step 14 (optional):

Provide a finished translation.

Step 15:

Write the paper.

Note well: As you go through the steps in this chapter, you need to be continually aware of the companion bibliography in Chapter IV. In some cases you will need to read widely in order to understand the distinctive features or nature of that step.

A. Initial Steps for All Genres

At the very beginning of the exegetical process, after you have determined the literary genre in which the text exists (see the Introduction), you need to have a provisional idea of what is going on, both in the whole document in general and in your own paragraph (or pericope) in particular. To do this well, several initial steps are necessary.

Step 1. Survey the historical context in general.

Before the investigation of any sentence, paragraph, or any other subsection of a document, one always needs to have a good sense about the entire document. Who is the author? Who are the recipients? What is the relationship between them? Where do the recipients live? What are their present circumstances? What historical situation occasioned this writing? What is the author's purpose? What is the overall theme or concern? Does the argument or narrative have an easily discerned outline?

It is to your great advantage, if time permits, to do this work for yourself; in a book study course this will be done in the process of the course. But for the exegesis of a "problem passage," you will often want to get right at the passage. Therefore, it is important to consult a content-oriented survey and a critical introduction (see IV.1).

Note: If you are approaching the text for reason 1, i.e., methodically working your way through a book (see Introduction), there is *no* substitute for doing this work for yourself. In this case you should do the following:

1.1. *Read the entire document through in English in one sitting.*

There is *no* substitute for this step. You never start exegeting a book at chapter 1, verse 1. The first step always is to read the entire document through. You need a provisional sense of the whole before analyzing any of its parts, and you gain such a sense by reading it through. [Note: One can read a letter the size of Philippians aloud (a good exercise, by the way) in about thirteen minutes, so one ought to read shorter documents through several times in successive days before starting on an exegesis project.]

After the first reading, go back through it a second time in skim fashion and make notes of the following (with references):

1.1.1. Discover everything you can about the recipients. Are they Jews or Gentiles? or a combination? What relation do they have with the author? Are there any hints of their socioeconomic situation?

1.1.2. Discover everything you can about the purpose. Does the author *explicitly* say anything about it? What is implied?

1.1.3. Note special emphases or concerns that emerge. What words or ideas are frequently repeated? What unusual vocabulary recurs? What, if anything, might these tell you about the occasion or purpose?

1.1.4. Work out an annotated outline of the whole book (to be revised on further study).

After you feel somewhat at home with the document as a whole, then proceed to the next steps.

1.2. *Check your observations against the secondary literature.*

Now go to the sources mentioned in Chapter IV and see whether there are some insights you missed. If there are significant differences between your observations and those in your NT Survey or Introduction, go back over the document with their book in hand to see what the reasons are for the differences.

Step 2. Confirm the limits of the passage.

Determine whether the passage you have chosen for exegesis is a genuine, self-contained unit. Even if you are exegeting only a single sentence, that sentence must be placed into its own paragraph or pericope. To do this, check the paragraphing of the two primary critical editions of the Greek text (NA[26] and UBS[3]; you will notice that they sometimes differ) against two or more modern translations (e.g., NRSV and NIV). Where any of these differ, you must tentatively decide for yourself what the basic unit is. The final decision on this matter will become a part of the whole exegetical process.

STEP 3. Become thoroughly acquainted with your paragraph/pericope.

NOTE WELL: For Steps 3 through 7, some differences in method exist for those who use Greek and those who do not. The special instructions for those who use English Bible only are found in brackets following the steps for those with Greek.

For those who use *Greek:* It would be to your great advantage also to read through the instructions for those who must work through the same procedures in the English Bible. If you are aiming toward, or are already involved in, professional ministry, you may find these materials helpful in teaching others within the church how to do the basic steps in the exegetical process.

For those who use *English:* Before skipping down to your part of the various steps, you should read through the part for Greek exegesis. This will give you an idea both as to what must be done for those who know the original language and what kinds of methodological differences exist for you. NOTE WELL: (1) Even though you may never learn Greek, it will be to your great advantage to learn the Greek alphabet; by so doing, you will be able to consult and use most of the better tools; (2) even if you cannot enter fully into the matters that have strictly to do with the Greek language, it is also to your great advantage to read as widely as possible from the bibliography in Chapter IV, so that you may at least understand the kinds of matters that are being discussed in the commentaries as you read them.

3.1. *Make a provisional translation.* [For English Bible see step 3.3]

The first essential matter is to become thoroughly acquainted with your paragraph. Nothing will help you do this better than to read through your paragraph in Greek and make a *provisional* translation. For rapid reading of the Greek, learn to use either Kubo, Rienecker-Rogers, or Zerwick-Grosvenor (see IV.3). Read the Greek text through several times, until you are sufficiently familiar with the *content* of the passage to be able to translate it without the lexical-grammatical aid. Then write out your translation, using your aid if you need to. Remember, this is not a finished translation. The purpose of this step primarily is to familiarize yourself with the *content* of your paragraph.

3.2. *Make a provisional list of exegetical difficulties.*

As you write out your translation, make a separate list of textual, grammatical, and lexical items that will need special study. For example, are there textual variations that make a difference in how one understands the text? Note especially any and all variations in the apparatus of UBS[3], since these were selected on the basis of their significance for translation. Which matters of grammar surfaced as you tried to translate? Which were noted in your translational aid (Rienecker-Rogers; Zerwick-Grosvenor)? Are there theologically loaded words? Are some words used repeatedly in this passage? Are there words in the passage that do not occur frequently in this author's writings?

NOTE: As a final step to your exegesis (Step 14), before the actual writing of the paper, you may be required to come back to this step and offer a finished translation, reflecting the conclusions of your exegesis. Even if you are not so required, it is good practice to learn to do this.

NOTE WELL: The next step (3.3) is the substitute step (for 3.1 and 3.2) for those without Greek; but those who use Greek may find it a very helpful exercise as well, so don't skip over it too quickly.

3.3. *Read the paragraph through in several translations.*

The best way for you to become acquainted with the paragraph and to discover what in the paragraph needs special study is to *read the paragraph through in at least seven translations*. As with the person using Greek, the aim of this exercise is to help you become thoroughly familiar with the paragraph, while at the same time discovering those places where further work will be needed in terms of Steps 5 through 7. To do this well, you will need to do the following:

3.3.1. Secure at least seven different translations (preferably the KJV, NASB, NRSV, NIV, GNB, REB, NJB [although any number of other modern translations will serve as well in place of the final three; see bibliography in IV.3 for these choices]). You may wish to photocopy the appropriate paragraph from each of the translations, so that you can freely mark them up if you choose to do so.

3.3.2. Mark well the differences between/among your translations. You may do this either with colored markers on your photocopies, or, preferably, by making a list of the differences and supporting translations at every point.

3.3.3. Determine which of these differences is exegetically significant. That is, determine which differences are merely synonyms or matters of taste, and which make a genuine difference in meaning. This is your way of getting at step 3.2 above, "Make a provisional list of exegetical difficulties." The point is that whenever translations have truly significant differences between/among them, this is a sure indication that some exegetical difficulty lies behind the differences. This step will become easier with much practice. But you should be prepared to include items such as the difference between "minister" and "servant" in a passage like 1 Tim. 4:6, since "minister" in English probably presupposes much more about Timothy's "office" than the actual data of the text allow.

3.3.4. Try to determine whether the differences are matters of textual criticism (Step 5), grammar (Step 6), or lexicography (Step 7). This will also come easier with practice. [You should note that most of the marginal notes in your translations (except for the NASB) reflect matters of textual criticism.]

STEP 4. Analyze sentence structures and syntactical relationships. (See II.1)

It is crucial very early on in the exegesis of your passage that you also have a good sense of the flow of the argument (or narrative) and that you recognize the basic structures and syntax of each sentence. To do this well there is no substitute for writing out the passage in its entirety in a structured form. There are three advantages to such a writing out of the passage. First, it forces you to make tentative grammatical decisions, especially about syntactical relationships. Second, it enables you to visualize the structure of the passage and to recognize patterns (e.g., resumptions, contrasts, parallels, chiasm). Third, it provides a tentative outline of the argument.

4.1. *Make a sentence flow.* (See II.1.1; pp. 65–80)

The best way to write out the text is in the form of a sentence flow, with marginal annotations tracing the flow of the argument. Although such work is a highly individual matter, the suggestions given in Chapter II can serve as useful guidelines.

[FOR ENGLISH BIBLE READERS: You should read carefully through the material in II.1. If you have difficulty with some of the grammatical/ syntactical concepts, read carefully the pages in Nunn, noted in IV.4. As you can see from the illustrations in II.1, this exercise can be performed in English as well as in Greek.]

4.2. *Make a sentence diagram.* (See II.1.2)

At times the grammar of a given sentence is so complex that it is useful to diagram its constituent parts. Many will prefer to diagram all the sentences of the passage, rather than to learn a new system, such as writing out a sentence flow. The advantage of the diagram is that it forces one to identify grammatically every word in the passage. The disadvantage is that one diagrams only one sentence at a time and thereby may fail to visualize the whole passage or to recognize various structural patterns in the argument.

As you complete these first four steps, two things should have happened:

a. You should now have a good idea about both the content and the larger context of the paragraph.
b. You should have isolated some of the problem areas that need closer examination.

You are now ready for a closer analysis of the passage (refer back to the provisional list in 3.2). The next four steps isolate the basic content questions that need resolution. Each of these steps is elaborated in detail in Chapter II. If you have already learned the procedures outlined in that chapter, then you simply need to work them out for the purposes of your paper. If not, then you will need to take the time to learn each of these procedures and see how they apply to your passage. Once the basic procedures are learned well, then Chapter II can serve as a handy reference guide or checklist.

[FOR ENGLISH BIBLE READERS: With Steps 5–7 (but not Step 8) you now come to the materials where you will need to consult outside help almost from the beginning. However, in order to make your secondary sources as useful as possible, you should do the following:

[a. Read as carefully as possible the materials in Chapter II, and as widely as possible the suggested overview readings in Chapter IV. Your concern here is for understanding, i.e., what scholarship itself is about in the three areas of textual criticism, grammar, and lexicography. You will be most limited in being able to do your own work at Steps 5 and 6 (text and grammar); but the limitation should be only one of not knowing the Greek language. You can come to understand the nature of textual and grammatical decisions as well as those who know the language, if you will read carefully from the suggested readings. Your concern here is to be able to enter into full understanding of the *reasons given for choices* in your commentaries or other secondary sources that discuss the exegetical questions in your passage.

[b. For the actual resolution of these matters you will need to look at several commentaries or other secondary sources (see the bibliography in IV.13). Here you need to read widely enough in order to get a good sense of the options, and the differences among scholars. You will quickly discover that some matters are more difficult to resolve than others. In the final analysis, here you must weigh the arguments of others pro and con, and then try to come to some resolution for yourself on the basis of their arguments. This is why you need first to follow the suggestion in (a) above, so as to become knowledgeable of the discipline and the issues being discussed.]

STEP 5.   Establish the text. (See II.2)

The first concern of the interpreter of any ancient text is the textual one. What words did the author use, and in what order? The science that seeks to recover the original form of hand-produced documents is called *textual criticism,* which has become a very technical and complex field of study. With a small amount of concerted effort, however, student exegetes can learn enough so as (1) to feel at home with textual discussions (e.g., in articles and commentaries) and (2) to feel somewhat comfortable in making their own textual decisions.

In order to do your own textual criticism, you will need to become familiar with the apparatuses (textual information in the footnotes) of both the NA[26] and UBS[3]. A full explanation of the use of these apparatuses and a discussion of the criteria for making textual choices are given in II.2.

What is emphasized in Chapter II needs to be noted here: Not all textual decisions have exegetical significance. But you need to become familiar enough with the science in order to be able both to discriminate what has significance from what does not and to evaluate the textual decisions of others for yourself. In the exegesis paper itself, only those textual decisions need be discussed that actually affect the *meaning* of the passage.

STEP 6. Analyze the grammar. (See II.1 and 3)

For your own purposes you should decide the grammar for everything in your passage. But again, in your paper discuss only those items where exegetical decision is important or makes a difference in the meaning of a passage. Are any grammatical points in doubt? Could any sentences, clauses, or phrases be read differently if the grammar were construed differently? Are there genuine ambiguities that make a definite interpretation of some part of the passage impossible? If so, what at least are the possible options? Is the grammar anomalous (not what would be expected) at any point? If so, can you offer any explanation for the anomaly?

STEP 7. Analyze significant words. (See II.4)

Be careful here. Do not let your paper become a collection of mini word studies. Discuss the meaning of any word in accordance with the guidelines in Chapter II. In your paper, discuss words on the basis of two criteria: (1) Explain what is not obvious. (2) Concentrate on key words and wordings.

STEP 8. Research the historical-cultural background.
(See II.5)

Involved in this step are a variety of concerns that include (1) the meaning of persons, places, events, etc., mentioned in the passage; (2) the cultural-social milieu of the author and his readers; (3) the customs and practices of the author or speaker and his readers or listeners; and (4) the thought world of the author and his readers.

In your paper, as before, you need to decide which of these matters need to be elaborated, on the basis of (1) what is not obvious to your readers, and (2) what makes a genuine difference in the meaning of the passage.

B. Special Considerations for Different Genres

At this point you are ready to wrestle with the questions of historical context (in particular) and literary context. However, the procedure here for exegeting the various genres differs considerably. The next steps, therefore, are discussed according to genre. At Step 12 all the genres return to the same track. It may be helpful at this point to refer frequently to the schematic diagram at the beginning of this chapter.

B (E). *Exegeting the Epistles*

Step 9 (E). Determine the formal character of the Epistle.

9.1 (E). *Differences in Character*

Although all the NT documents from Romans to Jude (21 in all) are Epistles, they have some considerable differences in character. Some are totally ad hoc, very specifically occasioned (e.g., Philemon, 1 Corinthians, Jude, Galatians), while others appear to be more like tracts at large. It is important at this point to be sensitive to the degree that some are more like real "letters" and some more public, and therefore real "epistles." This will especially affect your thinking at Step 10, having to do with the historical context in particular.

9.2 (E). *Formal Aspects*

It is also important to note the various *formal* aspects of the ancient letter and to determine to which part of the letter your passage belongs. For example, is it a part of the thanksgiving or prayer? Is it part of the formal greeting? Or is it part of the body proper? If it belongs to the more formal parts of the letter, how much has the form itself determined the content? Be sure to consult the bibliography in Chapter IV if you are not well acquainted with ancient literary practices, including such a common matter as letter writing.

9.3 (E). *Rhetorical Features*

To lesser or greater degrees the writers of the NT Epistles used the various rhetorical forms of the Greco-Roman world. In the case of Paul in particular one must be aware of these rhetorical devices, and ask oneself about both their nature and significance. Thus one needs to be aware of changes of mood or of forms of argumentation. Does your paragraph exhibit a sudden outburst of unanswered questions?

Does it display a sudden change in the form of argumentation? Is it primarily indicative, or imperative, or interrogative? Does the author seem to be engaging in "straight talk"? or perhaps irony? or hyperbole? Are there any of the elements of diatribe? Do any of the parts, or the whole itself, exhibit chiasm? Is your paragraph part of the argument, or is it appeal, or perhaps application? For these matters one must do some reading in the items listed in Chapter IV.

In some cases it is possible that the entire letter follows the patterns of classical rhetorical argumentation. Again, for these matters you will need to consult the bibliography in Chapter IV. Read widely enough to become acquainted with both the art and forms of ancient rhetoric. Then think through for yourself how much the *form* itself impacts the actual meaning of the text.

Step 10 (E).   Examine the historical context in particular.

Since the NT Epistles are all *occasional* documents (i. e., they were *occasioned* by some *special* circumstance either from the reader's side or from the author's), it is important to try to reconstruct the nature of the situation to which your major subsection of the letter is a response. To do this well one should attempt the following:

10.1 (E).   *Reading for Details*

Read the subsection through several times. As you read, pay close attention to the details of the text. As best you can, try to imagine what it would have been like to be sitting in an early Christian community hearing the letter read for the first time.

10.2 (E).   *Audience*

Make a list of everything you can that tells you something about *the recipients and their situation.* What is said explicitly? What is implied? Are they involved in behavior that needs correcting? Is the problem one of theological misunderstanding? or lack of understanding? Are they in need of comfort? exhortation? correction? If a specific problem is involved, has it come from outside the believing community or risen from within? Is there any hint as to how the author has learned of the situation?

10.3 (E).   *Key Words*

Make another list of *key words and repeated phrases* that indicate the subject matter of the section. What words appear most often in the whole section? Check your concordance to see whether there is an unusual incidence of them here. Does the author's vocabulary itself suggest anything about the nature of the problem?

10.4 (E). *Summary Description*

Try at this point, in a tentative way, to *write a paragraph that puts all these data into a coherent expression* of the problem or situation of the readers.

This step will usually be an important consideration in your final presentation of the exegesis. Be sure to come back to it after you have worked your way through Step 11, because your analysis of the answer should adequately correspond to your analysis of the historical situation.

Step 11 (E). Determine the literary context.

To do this, one must learn to THINK PARAGRAPHS. Even though your exegesis paper is keying in on only one of the paragraphs or subparagraphs in a larger section, you should try to trace the argument of the whole section, paragraph by paragraph.

For your specific text you have now come to the absolutely essential exegetical question: *What is the point* of this paragraph or exhortation? What is the point of this sentence? On the basis of what the author has said up to here, *why* does he now say this? This is why it is so important to trace the argument carefully right up to the point of your sentence or paragraph (although a full detailing of the whole argument does not need to be included in the paper itself). For exegesis it is not enough to work out all the details in Steps 5–8. One must also be able to offer a cogent explanation as to how all this fits into the author's ongoing argument.

To do this well, you should try to do two things:

11.1 (E). *Logic and Content*

In a compact way write out the *logic* and *content* of your paragraph. In your own words, *describe* (briefly!) *what* the author has said and *how* his argument develops.

The concern here is with *what* is being said. Who is now being addressed? What issue is now being spoken to? What is the absolutely central concern? Does your description include *everything* in the paragraph? Have you given proper weight to each item?

11.2 (E). *Content and Argument*

In another sentence or two explain *how* this content contributes to the argument.

The concern here is with the purpose or intent of the paragraph in the author's argument or flow of thought. Why do you think it is said right at this point? What is the relationship of this paragraph to what has just been said? How does it prepare for what is to come?

One cannot overemphasize the need for you to discipline yourself to do this exercise. No matter how well you do the details in the previous steps, you will never do good exegesis until you do this step well. The fault of most commentaries lies right here. They frequently handle the content questions well, but all too often fail to help the reader understand the *point* of the biblical author's words in a given context.

Before going on to Step 12 (p. 54), be sure to go back and think your way through Steps 10 and 11 together. Is your understanding of the answer an adequate response to the historical situation as you have described it? Does it now need some revision? Could you now make a convincing case for your exegesis as an adequate understanding of the situation to which the author is writing and his response to it? The excellence of your exegesis stands or falls here.

B (G). *Exegeting the Gospels*

Before going through the contextual questions for exegeting the Gospels, it is necessary to make some preliminary notes about the *nature* of this genre, which in turn requires the articulation of some prior working hypotheses about the materials in the Gospels and the interrelationships among the Gospels.

a. *The Nature of the Gospels*

The Epistles have basically a one-dimensional historical and literary context. That is, the author is presenting his own argument (or exhortation)—even when he draws on traditional material—that speaks directly to the situation of the recipients. Thus:

Paul (54 C.E.) ⟶ Corinth (54 C.E.)

The Gospel writers, by way of contrast, have a two- or three-dimensional historical context, which in turn affects their literary context. That is, they are handing on, now in the permanent form of writing, the sayings of and narratives about Jesus (level 1) that are available to them as they have been preserved in the church's tradition (level 2) [for example, compare 1 Cor. 11:23: "I handed on to you what I received" (written in 54 C.E.) with Luke 22:17–20 (written ca. 75 C.E.?)]. The Gospel writer's own contribution (level 3) is that of selectivity, arrangement, and adaptation (although such activity was already at work in the period of oral transmission). Thus:

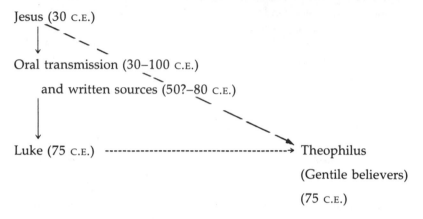

Jesus (30 C.E.)

Oral transmission (30–100 C.E.)

and written sources (50?–80 C.E.)

Luke (75 C.E.) --→ Theophilus

(Gentile believers)

(75 C.E.)

Thus it is *Jesus* with whom Theophilus is being brought face to face, but Jesus *mediated* through the memory of the early church and through Luke.

The exegetical process is further complicated (or perhaps aided) by the fact that there are four Gospels, the first three of which, at least, have some kind of literary interrelationship.

These two factors, that the Gospels are two- or three-dimensional and that there are four of them, require some prior working hypotheses about the Gospel materials and the Gospels themselves. The following hypotheses are the convictions of the author on which the various steps of exegesis will be predicated. It should be noted that they are the shared convictions of the vast majority of NT scholars. It should also be noted that it is not possible *not* to have working hypotheses on these matters—even if one has never articulated them. If you differ with these hypotheses, you of necessity will have to articulate your own, and adapt the steps accordingly.

b. *Some Working Hypotheses*

1. It is reasonable to assume that during the period of oral transmission the individual units of material (pericopes), composed of narratives and sayings, were transmitted largely independently of each other. Similarly, one may assume that many sayings were pre-

served as teaching per se and thus were frequently transmitted without their original historical context (cf. Paul's use of the sayings material in 1 Cor. 7:10 and 9:14). Thus it is a reasonable working hypothesis that the present arrangement of the pericopes is in large measure the work of the Evangelists themselves. This seems to be confirmed, to use but one example, by the fact that the sayings collected by Matthew in Matt. 10:5–42, as instructions for the ministers of the kingdom, are found in Luke in considerably different settings, in the following sequence: Luke 9:2–5; 10:3; 12:11–12; 6:40; 12:2–9; 12:51–53; 14:25–27; 17:33; 10:16.

2. Although no one of the Gospels was written to be read alongside the others (with the possible exception of John, according to Clement of Alexandria's view), it is almost certain that the Synoptic Gospels at least were not written independently of each other. Although three or four solutions to the Synoptic problem currently vie for acceptance, the view of the vast majority of scholars, and the one assumed in this book, is (a) that Mark was written first, (b) that Matthew and Luke *independently* used Mark in writing their own Gospels, and (c) that Matthew and Luke also had access to large quantities of other traditional materials, some of which they had in common (known as Q, but probably not a single, unified source).

3. The Evangelists themselves selected, arranged, and adapted the materials not simply to *record* or *preserve* the life and teachings of Jesus but also to *present* Jesus to their readers with their own distinctive concerns and from their distinctive points of view.

c. *The Task of Exegesis*

Given the nature of the Gospels and these three working hypotheses, it is further assumed that the task of exegesis is primarily to understand a passage in its present context in a given Gospel. But this has two aspects. First, the Evangelist is recording the life and teaching of *Jesus;* thus part of the task is to try to see what the Evangelist understood to have been said or to have happened. But second, since he selected/adapted/arranged in *this* way, we also want to try to see its meaning in the present context of the Gospel. Thus, the primary task of exegesis is not to reconstruct a Life of Jesus, but to interpret a passage within its present literary context in a given Gospel, taking into consideration, of course, what one knows from other passages about the "life of Jesus."

The alternative to this view of the task is to concentrate on a pericope or saying per se in an attempt to understand what it meant in the original setting of Jesus. As you will see by what follows, this is an important part of the exegetical task, but it is only a halfway house if one does not in fact move back to the Gospels themselves, since this is the only *certain* context one has.

With these preliminary matters in view, we may now proceed to the actual steps in the exegetical process.

STEP 9 (G).   Determine the formal character of the pericope or saying.

For this section especially you will need to consult the bibliography in Chapter IV. The outline assumes a certain amount of knowledge of these matters.

9.1 (G).   *Identify the general literary type.*

Is your pericope or sentence a narrative or a saying? Or is it a combination of the two—a pronouncement story? Each of these types functions in a different way.

9.2 (G).   *Identify the specific literary form.*

9.2.1.   If your pericope is a *narrative*, is it a miracle story? Does it have all the formal characteristics of such stories? Is it a story *about* Jesus? Or about John the Baptist? About such a narrative you might ask, why was it preserved in the tradition? What important thing about Jesus does it tell you by the very fact of its preservation? More importantly, how does the narrative now function in the Evangelist's narrative? To reinforce a teaching? As one in a series that illustrate some aspect of Jesus' mission or message?

9.2.2.   If your passage is a *saying*, what kind of saying is it? Is it a parable? a similitude? an apocalyptic saying? a wisdom saying? a prophetic utterance? a piece of legal material? Does it have poetic elements? chiasm? Does it employ overstatement? irony? metaphor? paradox? How much does the analysis of form help you to identify audience? How much does it play a part in understanding? For example, a proverb with metaphors like Matt. 24:28 ("Wherever the body is, there the eagles will be gathered together," RSV) is *not* intended to be allegorized. The whole proverb has a *single* point, and the metaphor of carcass and vultures is trying to point to a reality about the consummation of the kingdom. The exegetical question is, *What* is it saying about the consummation? Suddenness? Inevitability? Visibility?

STEP 10 (G).   **Analyze the pericope in a Gospel synopsis.**
               (See II.6)

Because each of the Gospel writers selected, arranged, and adapted the traditional material available to him, it is important for the exegesis of any one of the Gospels to see the pericope in your Gospel as it is related to the other Gospels. To do this one must learn to use a Gospel synopsis, as outlined in II.6.

This analysis consists of three questions. (NOTE: "Triple tradition" means the pericope is found in Mark-Matthew-Luke; "double tradition" means Matthew-Luke; "single tradition" means it is found in only one of the Gospels—Matthew or Luke.)

10.1 (G). *Selectivity*

This question has simply to do with the fact that the pericope *is* found in your Gospel. Is it also found in one or more of the others? Is its inclusion related to the known special interests of the Evangelist?

10.2 (G). *Arrangement*

The question here has to do with its present literary context. Here in particular, as with 10.3 (G), you need to consult Chapter II. These steps are important because they are the keys to the prism through which the Evangelist is viewing Jesus and his teaching.

The question of arrangement is: Why is the saying (pericope) included *here?* Is it in the same context in the other Gospel(s)? If different, is it in a similar or different *kind* of context (i.e., eschatological, teaching on discipleship, etc.)? Does the present context, in comparison with the other(s), tell you something about the Gospel writer's own special interests?

One must be careful here. It is altogether possible that an Evangelist included a pericope at a given point simply because it was already in that context in the tradition itself (see, e.g., how much of Mark the other Evangelists did not rearrange!); and therefore he may "mean" nothing by its present arrangement. In this regard one needs to exercise proper caution about Mark and John. That is, they too may have followed sequences already available in their sources and therefore may not always have special meaning to their arrangement. On the other hand, since the vast majority of materials (mostly sayings) in the double tradition are not in sequence, one may assume the same thing regularly also to be true of Mark and John (i.e., that the sequencing is their own).

10.3 (G). *Adaptation*

The question here has to do with isolating the author's own adaptation of the pericope to his own Gospel from the traditional material he had available to him. Again, you need to consult Chapter II (II.6.3 and 6.6).

Has your author added or omitted anything? What verbal changes has he made? Are they merely stylistic? Are they more substantive? Do the changes reveal the author's interests? his unique emphases? Does the adaptation of your pericope align with a series of such changes, either in the larger context of your pericope itself or in the whole Gospel?

You will recognize as you complete this part of the exegesis that you have been wrestling with the questions of both the literary context and the historical context of the Evangelist himself. That is, why does he include this pericope right at this point with these special emphases? But there is one other factor that needs to be considered—the historical context of Jesus himself.

STEP 11 (G). Consider possible life settings in the ministry of Jesus.

The concern here has to do especially with the sayings (teaching) of Jesus, since so many of them were transmitted in the oral tradition apart from their original historical context and have been given their present literary context by the Evangelists themselves. It is therefore of some exegetical importance to analyze the sayings as to their possible life setting in the ministry of Jesus himself.

This analysis can best be done in terms of audience. Given the nature of the *content* of the saying, was it most likely spoken originally to the disciples? to the crowds? to the Pharisees? Is the saying best understood in the context of conflict? of discipleship?

Many times, of course, it will not be possible to determine this and one must simply accept the present context of the Gospels. But in cases, for example, where Matthew or Luke have inserted something into the Markan framework, or where Matthew and Luke have identical materials in two different settings, one may frequently isolate the material and on the basis of content offer a very plausible original life setting for the saying. But note carefully:

    a. This is the most speculative part of the exegetical task, so learn to err on the side of caution.

b. To recover the meaning in the life setting of Jesus is *not* the primary aim of exegesis. Rather the primary aim is to determine the meaning of the text in its *present* literary context. But the life setting of Jesus himself must be a part of the total picture.

B (A). *Exegeting Acts*

Exegesis of the Acts can be difficult for both students and pastors because of the kinds of concerns one brings to the book. Those concerns are basically of two kinds: historical (what actually was happening in the life of the early church?) and theological/hermeneutical (what did all of this mean, and what does it mean for us today?). Good exegesis must be a combination of the historical and theological, without being predetermined by the hermeneutical question.

It is especially crucial in exegeting Acts to go back to Step 1 and have a good grasp of Luke's purpose. Such a careful review is a must before proceeding further and will correspond somewhat to Steps 9 (E) and 9 (G). The next two steps then cover the historical and "theological" concerns just noted.

Step 10 (A). Research the historical questions.

In reality, this step is very similar to step 11.1 (E) for the Epistles. The concern here is with *what* is being said, and therefore also includes some of the content questions from Steps 5–8. Thus in a compact way you should try to write out *what* precisely Luke has told us in a given narrative. Who are the main characters in the narrative? What are they now doing? Are there any persons, places, or other names or ideas that you should look up in your Bible dictionary?

Step 11 (A). Determine the literary context.

Now we come to the crucial matter for the exegesis of Acts. What is the point of this narrative or speech? How is it related to what has just been narrated? How does it function in Luke's total narrative? Why has he included it here (the question of selectivity)? Are there any peculiarities in the narrative or speech, in comparison with others in Acts, that may give clues to Luke's special interests here?

Before moving on to Steps 12–15, one should note two cautions in exegeting Acts:

1. The speeches, by and large, may be exegeted very much like the Epistles. However, it must be noted that in their *present* form they reflect Lukan style and vocabulary (very much like Luke's rewriting of Mark). Therefore, in the style of Hellenistic historians, following Thucydides, Luke reports what essentially was said at a given point, but he himself has written the speech in its present form. Here especially, then, the contextual question—why is a speech included here—is a very important one.

2. One must be extremely cautious of overexegeting Acts either by making too much of silence (how Luke did *not* say something) or by assuming that absolute precision was being sought after. It is the nature of Hellenistic historians to paint vivid pictures of real events and not necessarily to offer the dry chronicle of a police report. This is history that is also story.

B (R). *Exegeting the Book of Revelation*

The Revelation has all too often been a closed book, partly because of the inherent difficulties with the apocalyptic mold in which it is cast and partly because so much speculative application has been made by people who do not understand apocalyptic.

Because of our general lack of acquaintance with the literary form of the Revelation, you would do well in this case to consult two or three good commentaries as you do your own work. You should perhaps have all three of the following:

> George R. Beasley-Murray, *The Book of Revelation*; New Century Bible (Grand Rapids: Wm. B. Eerdmans Publishing Co., 1978).
> Isbon T. Beckwith, *The Apocalypse of St. John* (New York: Macmillan Co., 1919; repr. Grand Rapids: Baker Book House, 1967).
> Robert H. Mounce, *The Book of Revelation*; New International Commentary (Grand Rapids: Wm. B. Eerdmans Publishing Co., 1977).

STEP 9 (R). Understand the formal character of the Revelation.

Before exegeting any single vision (or letter) in the Revelation, you need a good understanding of the formal literary character of the book, which is a unique, finely blended combination of three distinct literary types: apocalypse, prophecy, and letter. On this matter, read Beasley-Murray, pp. 12–29.

Since the apocalyptic *images* are often the most difficult items for exegesis, some special words need to be added here, which offer proper guidelines and cautions.

9.1 (R). *Determine the source or background of the image.*

Here you will do well to consult Beckwith or Beasley-Murray. Is this image related to the OT? Is it used elsewhere in apocalyptic? ancient mythology? contemporary culture? Is the image a standard image of apocalyptic? Or is it a "fluid" image (like the lion–lamb in Rev. 5, or the two women in Rev. 12 and 17)?

9.2 (R). *Determine the present use of the image.*

Is the present use by John identical with, or different from, its source? Has it been "broken" and thus transformed into a new image? Are there any internal clues as to John's intent in the use of the image? Does John himself interpret the image? If so, hold this firmly as a starting point for understanding others. Does the image refer to something general, or is it intended to refer to some specific thing or event?

9.3 (R). *See the visions as wholes.*

One must be extremely careful to see the visions as "whole cloth" and not allegorically press all the details. In this matter the visions are like the parables. The whole vision is trying to say something; the details are either (*a*) for dramatic effect (Rev. 6:12–14) or (*b*) to add to the picture of the whole so that the readers will not mistake the points of reference (Rev. 9:7–11). Thus the details of the sun turning black like sackcloth and the stars falling like late figs probably do not "mean" anything. They simply make the whole vision of the earthquake more impressive. However, in 9:7–11 the locusts with crowns of gold, human faces, and women's long hair help to fill out the picture in such a way that the original readers could hardly have mistaken what was in view—the barbarian hordes at the outer edges of the Roman Empire.

STEP 10 (R). Determine the historical context.

It is especially important that one recognize also the epistolary and prophetic elements in the Revelation. Thus as one approaches any single vision (or letter), one must always be aware of the two foci—the persecution of the church, on the one hand, and the judgment of God against the persecutors, on the other. The letters and the visions depicting the church's suffering belong to the history of the author and his readers. The visions of God's coming wrath are, in typically prophetic fashion, to be held in tension between history and eschatology (temporal judgment against the backdrop of eschatological judgment).

On the question of the historical situation and the purpose of the book, you should read Beckwith, pp. 197–216.

STEP 11 (R).   Determine the literary context.

To determine the literary context of any vision, you must first work out for yourself an adequate frame of reference for the whole. The Revelation for the most part is easily outlined in its major sections (chs. 1–3, 4–5, 6–7, 8–11, 12–14, 15–16, 17–18, 19–22). One of the major exegetical questions has to do with how these sections are related to each other so as to form the whole. On this matter, read Beasley-Murray, pp. 29–32, and Mounce, pp. 45–49.

After that, the question of the literary context of any letter or vision, or part thereof, is precisely as it is with the Epistles (Step 11 [E]).

C. FURTHER STEPS COMMON TO ALL

STEP 12.   Consider the broader biblical and theological contexts.

As you begin to draw together all of your discoveries and especially begin to focus on the point, or "message," of your passage, you will want to fit it into its broader biblical and theological contexts.

How does the passage function dogmatically (i.e., as teaching or conveying a message) in the section, book, division, Testament, Bible—in that order? How does it or its elements compare to other Scriptures that address the same sorts of issues? To what is it similar or dissimilar? What hinges on it elsewhere? What other elements in Scripture help make it comprehensible? Why? How? Does the passage affect the meaning or value of other Scriptures in a way that crosses literary or historical lines? What would be lost or how would the message of the Bible be less complete if the passage did not exist?

Similarly theologically, where does the passage fit within the whole corpus of revelation comprising Christian (dogmatic) theology? To what doctrine or doctrines does the passage relate? What in fact are the problems, blessings, concerns, confidences, etc., about which the passage has something to say? How does the passage speak to these? How clearly are they dealt with in the passage? Is the passage one that raises apparent difficulties for some doctrines while solving others? If so, try to deal with this situation in a manner that is helpful to your readers.

What does the passage contain that contributes to the solution of doctrinal questions or supports solutions offered elsewhere in Scripture? How major or minor is the passage's contribution? How certain can you be that the passage, properly understood, has the theological significance you propose to attach to it? Does your approach agree with that of other scholars or theologians who are known to have addressed themselves to the passage?

STEP 13. Accumulate a bibliography of secondary sources and read widely.

13.1. *Investigate what others have said about the passage.*

Even though you will have consulted commentaries, grammars, and many kinds of other books and articles in the process of completing the preceding steps, you should now undertake a more systematic investigation of the secondary literature that may apply to your exegesis. In order for the exegesis to be your work and not merely a mechanical compendium of others' views, it is wise to do your own thinking and to arrive at your own conclusions as much as possible prior to this step. Otherwise, you are not so much doing an exegesis of the passage as you are evaluating others' exegeses—and therefore helping to guarantee that you will not go beyond that which they have achieved.

Now, however, is the proper time to ask what various scholars think about the passage. (For the accumulation of your bibliography, see Chapter IV.) As you read, be alert to the following questions: What points have they made that you overlooked? What have they said better? What have they given more weight to? Can you point out things that they have said that are questionable or wrong? If in your opinion other commentators are incorrect, point this out, using the footnotes for minor differences and the body of the paper for more significant ones.

13.2. *Compare and adjust.*

Have the conclusions of other scholars helped you to change your analysis in any way? Do they attack the passage or any aspects of it in a manner that is more incisive or that leads to a more satisfying set of conclusions? Do they organize their exegesis in a better way? Do they give attention to implications you hadn't even considered? Do they supplement your own findings? If so, do not hesitate to revise your own conclusions or procedures in the preceding steps, giving proper credit in each case. But never feel that you must cover in your exegesis everything that the others do. Reject what does not seem germane, and limit what seems out of proportion. You decide, not they.

NOTE: A student is not bound to reproduce slavishly the interpretations of others, but you *are* bound to assess critically what you read. Before one can say, "I disagree," one must be able to say, "I understand." It is axiomatic that before you level criticism you should be able to state an author's position in terms that he or she would find acceptable. After that you may proceed in any of six directions:

a. Show where the author is *misinformed.*
b. Show where the author is *uninformed.*
c. Show where the author is *inconsistent.*
d. Show where the author's treatment is *incomplete.*
e. Show where the author *misinterprets* through faulty assumptions or procedures.
f. Show where the author *makes valuable contributions* to the discussion at hand.

13.3. *Apply your discoveries throughout your paper.*

Do not include a separate section of findings from secondary literature in any draft of your paper. Do not view this step as resulting in a single block of material within the paper. Your discoveries should produce additions or corrections, or both, at many points throughout the exegesis. Try to be sure that a change or addition at one point does not contradict statements made elsewhere in the paper. Consider the implications of all changes. For example, if you adjust the textual analysis on the basis of your evaluation of something in the secondary literature, how will this affect the translation, lexical data, and other parts of the exegesis? Aim for consistency and evenness throughout. This will affect considerably the reader's ability to appreciate your conclusions.

13.4. *Know when to quote.*

One of the common difficulties with student papers is a strong tendency to overquote. For the most part the use of quotation should be limited to the following four instances:

13.4.1. Quote when it is necessary or important to use the very words of an author so as not to misrepresent.

13.4.2. Quote when it is necessary for a clear or convincing presentation of an option.
   Many times a quotation of this kind will stand at the beginning of a section or paragraph as a point of departure.

13.4.3. Quote when it is useful for the psychological impact on the reader.
   For example, it is often useful to quote some well-known authority who holds the opinion you are contending for. Sometimes this is especially helpful if what is said may be contrary to one's ordinary expectations.

13.4.4. Quote when an author clearly says something better than you could, or when it is said in a clearly memorable way.

13.5. *Know the uses of annotation.*

One must learn to give due credit to secondary sources in footnotes (or endnotes or backnotes [notes on the back of the preceding typewritten page]) and bibliography. It is axiomatic, of course, that one *always* documents a *quote* or *reference* to an opinion or source. Notes may also be used—often to make your essay more readable or to show that it is more fully informed—in the following instances:

13.5.1. Use notes to list additional bibliographical material.
   This helps your reader to know that you are aware of others who share the same or similar opinion(s). It will also give the reader further help for his or her own independent study.

13.5.2.   Use notes to compare differing opinions.

Sometimes of course it is crucial to your paper to cite differing opinions in the body of your text. But frequently such differences may be explained more conveniently in the notes.

13.5.3.   Use notes to acknowledge technical difficulties that are important but beyond the scope of the paper or beside the immediate point.

13.5.4.   Use notes to develop peripheral arguments or implications.

13.5.5.   Use notes to display longer lists of primary source citations or references or for diagrams.

13.5.6.   Use notes to refer to another section of the paper.

STEP 14.   **Provide a finished translation** (optional).

After your research is complete and you are ready to write the final draft, place the finished translation immediately following the text. Use annotations (footnotes) to explain choices of wording that might be surprising or simply not obvious to your reader. You are not obliged, however, to explain any word that was also chosen by several modern versions. Use the footnotes to tell the reader other possible translations of a word or phrase that you consider to have merit. Do this especially wherever you find it difficult to choose between two or more options.

STEP 15.   **Write the paper.**

While it is true that there may be many acceptable formats for the actual writing of the paper, the following guidelines represent the basic logic of the paper—and may be followed with some confidence.

15 (E).   *For the Epistles*

15.1 (E).   *Problems*

If the passage is a "problem passage," or one that has known differences of opinion, the problem or differences of opinion should be set out in the first paragraph or two. Keep this brief, but be complete enough that the reader will have a good overview of the issues.

15.2 (E). *Contexts*

Otherwise the opening paragraphs should set your passage into both its historical and literary contexts.

  a. Give the historical context first—but do not spend a lot of time, if any, on matters of general introduction. Describe the historical situation as much as necessary—but do not make this the whole paper!
  b. Trace the argument up to your passage. *Very briefly* (don't reinvent the wheel!) set out the overall argument, then specifically indicate the steps that lead to your paragraph.

15.3 (E). *Overview*

Then present an overview of your passage. What is the *point* of this paragraph? What is its own logic and contribution to the argument? (You will note that this is basically a rewriting of Step 11 [E], above.)

15.4 (E). *Argument*

Finally, trace the argument itself in some detail, judiciously determining what from Steps 5–8 needs to be made a part of the body of the paper and what needs to be referred to in a footnote.

15.5 (E). *Conclusion*

Conclude in whatever way you can best tie the whole together.

15 (G). *For the Gospels*

The writing task here is most often determined by what kind of pericope or saying one is dealing with.

15.1 (G). *Opening*

Usually the opening will be problem oriented, and sometimes will include a summary of scholarly options.

15.2 (G). *Context*

In coming to the pericope or saying itself, one should usually begin by determining, if possible, whether the present literary context is the responsibility of the Evangelist or the tradition (i.e., one should note carefully where and how it appears in other Gospels).

15.3 (G). *Sitz im Leben Jesu*

Next you should discuss from the literature the various theories, or ramifications, as to the life setting of Jesus. This will often include:

a. A discussion pro and con of authenticity.
b. The various matters of content (text, words, etc.), including especially the historical-cultural background.
c. A discussion of the probable "original" form of the material, especially the sayings.

But do not spend an inordinate amount of time on (*a*) and (*b*). For example, in most exegesis papers one may assume authenticity if one is so disposed, but it is then proper to add a footnote to acknowledge those scholars who may think otherwise, and why.

15.4 (G). *Meaning*

Finally, one must discuss the meaning of the pericope in its present form and context, including a discussion of its meaning as the Evangelist has used it. This, after all, is the canonical level and is the "meaning" that is to be proclaimed.

D. THE APPLICATION

In some seminary courses, you will also be asked to include a sermon, or a sermon précis, with your exegesis. In that event you come to the task that is at once more difficult and more rewarding— moving from the first century to the present century, without abandoning your exegesis, on the one hand, but without rehashing it (as though that were preaching), on the other. The task is to take the *point* (or the several points) of the passage as you have exegeted it and to make *that* point a living word for a present-day congregation. This requires a lively imagination and the hard work of thinking, as well as the skill of having done the exegesis well. Since preaching is both art and event, as well as solid exegesis, there are no "rules" for writing the sermon. But here are some suggestions.

1. Biblical preaching from the New Testament is, by definition, the task of bringing about an encounter between people of today with the Word of God that was first spoken in the first century. The task of the exegete is to discover that Word and its meaning to the first-century church; the task of the preacher is to know well the people to whom that Word is now to be spoken again. Thus, good sermons will begin at either place: (1) with the biblical text that is

then brought to bear on the people (but this must be done with consummate skill so as not to bore the people to death till you get to where they are), or (2) with the needs of the people to which this text is going to speak (this tends to be the "safer" route).

2. Before writing out the sermon, one should sit down and hammer out three things—in writing—as guidelines for the sermon:

a. The *main point or points* of the biblical text that you want to proclaim. [CAUTION: Do not feel compelled to touch every exegetical point—only those that contribute to *this* sermon.]

b. The *purpose* of the present sermon, i.e., how the above points are seen to be applicable.

c. The *response* that one hopes the sermon will achieve.

3. By now an outline should have emerged. You will do well to write out the outline and keep it in view, along with the three guidelines, as you write.

4. If the course requirement calls for a précis, or summary, do all of the above, and give enough of the content so that your professor can not only see your outline but "feel" the urgency of your message.

II

EXEGESIS
AND THE ORIGINAL TEXT

THIS CHAPTER IS FILLED WITH a whole variety of aids to exegesis, which must be worked in at various points in the process outlined in Chapter I. The purpose for doing this in a second chapter is twofold: (1) to keep the student exegete from getting bogged down with details in Chapter I, lest there one fail to see the forest for the trees; and (2) to offer a real "how to" approach to these components—how to read the textual apparatus of the Greek text, how to get the most possible good from an entry in Bauer's *Lexicon*, and so on.

For many, going through this material will be like the experience of a Pentecostal trying to worship in a liturgical church. At the beginning, such a person can hardly worship because he or she doesn't know when to turn the page or when to kneel. But once the proper kinetic responses are learned, then one can concentrate on worship itself. So it is here. These details must be learned. At first they will seem to get in the way, or perhaps worse, seem to be the whole—or most significant part—of the process. But once they are learned well, the times "to stand or kneel" will become more automatic.

In contrast to Chapter I, here we will give several *examples* of how to go about the process. In fact, the various sections of this chapter are intended to function something like a manual; this means that the sections are not "easy reading," any more than any manual is. Each of the sections is written with the intent that you should (1) have "hands on" experience with the various methods and tools, and (2) therefore work with the tools themselves, not simply read about them here.

Those without knowledge of Greek will find that they can work with most of these materials, except for Sections 2 and 3. For Section 2 you are encouraged to read carefully the bibliographic items noted at the beginning. If you have learned the Greek alphabet, you should also be able to make your way through this section for yourself—at least to see what actually goes into the process. Section 3 is the one part where you cannot work without knowledge of the language. But again, the section has been written so that if you make yourself well acquainted with grammatical terminology and then read the section through slowly and carefully, you will be able to glean a great deal, and especially to have a basic understanding of grammatical discussions in the commentaries as you read them.

Sections 1, 4, 5, and 6 can all be done by those without Greek. I do not say that it will be easy going; but if you wish to learn the exegetical process, you must be able to do these various steps. Thus you might as well learn to do it in the same way as those who work with the original language. Much experience with these methods and materials in the classroom has made it abundantly clear that students without Greek who are intent to learn how to do exegesis do all of these steps just as well as those who work with the language.

Note well: In contrast to the way you read most books, where section headings are skipped over to go immediately to the reading of the material, in this chapter *you will need to read the* titles *of each section and subsection with care.* In most cases they also serve as the topic sentence for the succeeding paragraph(s).

For Sections 2 to 4, you should also be aware of an especially helpful book which guides you through all the resource tools and shows you how to use them:

Cyril J. Barber, *Introduction to Theological Research* (Chicago: Moody Press, 1982).

Section II.1

The Structural Analysis (See I.4)

THE PURPOSE OF STEP 4 in the exegetical process is to help you to visualize the structures of your paragraph and the flow of the argument, as well as to force you to make some preliminary grammatical decisions (on questions of grammar, and how *syntax* is involved, see below in Section II.3). What you are after here is the big picture, the *syntactical* relationships of the various words and word groups. In Section 3, below, we will examine the various grammatical questions related to morphology—the significance of case, tense, etc. (exegetical Step 6).

Since the present process is something of an individualized matter, there is no right or wrong here. But the procedure outlined below can be of immense and lifelong benefit if you will take the time to learn it well. Obviously, you may—and should—adapt it to your own style. Whatever you do must finally be practical and useful to you.

1.1. *Make a sentence flow.*

Probably the most helpful form of structural analysis is to produce a sentence flow schematic. This is a simplified form of diagraming, whose purpose is to depict graphically by coordination, and by indentation and subordination, the relation between words and clauses in a passage. One begins in the upper left margin with the subject and predicate of the first main clause and allows the paragraph to "flow" toward the right margin by lining up coordinate elements under one another and indenting subordinate or modifying elements. A sentence flow analysis, therefore, will include the following steps (1.1.1 through 1.1.5, below), which will be illustrated primarily from 1 Cor. 2:6–7.

[THOSE WITHOUT GREEK should be able to follow the process without too much difficulty. For your convenience we have included very literal and "wooden" English "translations." Thus, even without Greek you should be able to follow the procedure (provided, of course, that you know something about English grammar!). You will find this a helpful exercise, even from an English translation, provided that you use one of the more literal translations, such as the NASB or NRSV—although even here some of the syntactical decisions will have been made for you. Therefore, you may find it useful to consult a Greek-English interlinear, where an English equivalent appears above (or below) each Greek word of a provided Greek text. See, as the best example:

J. D. Douglas (ed.), *The New Greek-English Interlinear New Testament* (Wheaton, Ill.: Tyndale House Publishers, 1990).

[NOTE: You will probably want to do your initial work on scratch paper, so that you can arrange and rearrange the sentences, until you *see* the coordinations, balances, subordinations, contrasts, etc.]

1.1.1. *Start with the subject, predicate, and object.*

It is usually most helpful to begin at the top left corner with the subject (if expressed) and predicate of the first main clause along with the object (or predicate noun). In most instances it is helpful to rearrange the Greek into the standard English order: subject-verb-object. Thus in 1 Cor. 2:6 one should begin the first line as follows:

λαλοῦμεν σοφίαν	(It is not imperative that one rearrange
We speak wisdom	the word order, but you will notice when you come to v. 7 that these words are repeated, and you will want to present them as coordinate elements.)

There are two exceptions to this ordinary procedure:

a. One should be careful not to destroy an author's emphases or chiasms achieved by word order. Thus 1 Cor. 6:1 should begin:

τολμᾷ τις ὑμῶν
Dare any one of you?

and in 1 Cor. 3:17 one will probably wish to keep Paul's chiastic structure (subject-object-verb/verb-object-subject):

(A)	(B)	(C)	(B)	(A)
εἴ τις	τὸν ναὸν	φθείρει		
	τοῦ θεοῦ			
		φθερεῖ	τοῦτον	ὁ θεός

If anyone	the temple	destroys		
	of God			
		will destroy	this one	God

b. The last example also illustrates the second exception, namely, when the author's sentence *begins* with an adverb clause (especially εἰ, ἐάν, ὅτε, ὅταν, ὡς; if, when, since), it is usually best to begin the flow with this clause—even though grammatically it is a subordinate unit.

1.1.2. *Subordinate by indentation.*

One should subordinate by indentation all adverbial modifiers (i.e., adverbs, prepositional phrases [including most genitives], participial phrases, other adverb clauses), adjective clauses, and noun clauses; preferably under the word or word group being modified.

a. *Adverbs* (example: 1 Thess. 1:2):

εὐχαριστοῦμεν   τῷ θεῷ
               πάντοτε

We give thanks   to God
               always

b. *Prepositional phrases* (example: 1 Cor. 2:6):

λαλοῦμεν   σοφίαν
   ἐν τοῖς τελείοις

We speak   wisdom
   among the mature

c. *Genitives* (example: 1 Cor. 2:6):

σοφίαν
   οὐ   τοῦ αἰῶνος τούτου
   οὐδὲ   τῶν ἀρχόντων
             τοῦ αἰῶνος τούτου

wisdom
    not   of this age
    nor   of the rulers
             of this age

NOTE WELL: Unlike the sentence diagram, an adjective or possessive pronoun in most cases (as in the above example) will naturally accompany the noun it modifies.

d. *Adverbial participles* (example: 1 Thess. 1:2):

εὐχαριστοῦμεν . . .
    ποιούμενοι μνείαν

We give thanks . . .
    when we make mention

e. *Adverb clause* (example: 1 Cor. 1:27):

ὁ θεὸς   ἐξελέξατο τὰ μωρὰ
                τοῦ κόσμου
        <u>ἵνα</u>   (See 1.1.4 below
                                      for conjunctions)

    καταισχύνῃ τοὺς σοφούς

God   chose the foolish things
            of the world
        <u>in order that</u>
    he might shame the wise

f. *Adjective clause* (example: 1 Cor. 2:6, where an attributive participle functions as an adjective clause):

τῶν ἀρχόντων   of the rulers
    τοῦ αἰῶνος τούτου   of this age
    <u>τῶν</u> καταργουμένων   <u>who</u> are being set aside

g. *Noun clause* (example: 1 Cor. 3:16, where the ὅτι clause functions as the object of the verb):

οὐκ οἴδατε <u>ὅτι</u>
        ἐστὲ ναὸς
            τοῦ θεοῦ;

Do you not know <u>that</u>
        you are the temple
            of God?

Note well: In narratives, where one has direct discourse, the whole direct discourse functions similarly—as the object of the verb of speaking. Thus Mark 4:11:

ἔλεγεν αὐτοῖς·
            τὸ μυστήριον   δέδοται
                τῆς βασιλείας   ὑμῖν

He was saying to them:
            The mystery   is given
                of the kingdom   to you

h. *Infinitives* create some difficulties here. The basic rule is: If the infinitive is complementary, keep it on the same line as its modal; if it functions as a verbal or nominal clause, subordinate as with other clauses. Thus 1 Cor. 3:1:

κἀγὼ οὐκ ἠδυνήθην   λαλῆσαι
                            ὑμῖν

And I was not able   to speak
                          to you

but 1 Cor. 2:2:

ἔκρινα
        εἰδέναι   οὔ τι
        ἐν ὑμῖν

I determined
        to know   not a thing
        among you

1.1.3. *Coordinate by lining up.*

One should try to visualize all coordinations (e.g., coordinate clauses, phrases, and words, or balanced pairs or contrasts) by lining them up directly under one another, even if at times such coordinate elements appear much farther down in the sentence or paragraph. Note the following illustrations:

1 Cor. 2:6 and 7 should begin at the left margin:

λαλοῦμεν σοφίαν   We speak wisdom
    | |

λαλοῦμεν σοφίαν   We speak wisdom

In the οὐ . . . οὐδὲ (not . . . nor) phrases of v. 6, one may present the balance in one of two ways, either by coordinating the two genitives themselves:

σοφίαν
     οὐ   τοῦ αἰῶνος τούτου
     οὐδὲ   τῶν ἀρχόντων
                   τοῦ αἰῶνος τούτου

wisdom
     not   of this age
     nor   of the rulers
                    of this age

or by coordinating the phrase "of this age," which occurs again at the end of v. 7:

σοφίαν
     οὐ   τοῦ αἰῶνος τούτου
     οὐδὲ   τῶν ἀρχόντων
                   τοῦ αἰῶνος τούτου

wisdom
     not   of this age
     nor   of the rulers
               of this age

At 1.1.2e above, you will note that we subordinated ἵνα (in order that), but lined up ἐξελέξατο τὰ μωρά (he chose the foolish things) and καταισχύνῃ τοὺς σοφούς (he might shame the wise). In this way the intended contrasts are immediately made visible.

NOTE: The problem of coordination and subordination is more complex when there are several elements that modify the same word(s), but which themselves are not coordinate. Thus in 1 Cor. 2:7 there are two prepositional phrases that both modify προώρισεν (he predetermined) but are not themselves coordinate. Here again is a matter of personal preference. Either coordinate:

ὁ θεὸς προώρισεν   God predetermined
     πρὸ τῶν αἰώνων   before the ages
     εἰς δόξαν ἡμῶν   for our glory

or place the second item slightly to the left of the first (so as not to suggest subordination of one to the other):

ὁ θεὸς προώρισεν	God predetermined
πρὸ τῶν αἰώνων	before the ages
εἰς δόξαν ἡμῶν	for our glory

NOTE: Coordinate conjunctions between words or phrases can be set apart, either between the lines or to the left, but this should be done as unobtrusively as possible. Thus 1 Cor. 2:3, either:

ἐν ἀσθενείᾳ	in weakness
καὶ	and
ἐν φόβῳ	in fear
καὶ	and
ἐν τρόμῳ πολλῷ	in much trembling

or:

	ἐν ἀσθενείᾳ		in weakness
καὶ	ἐν φόβῳ	and	in fear
καὶ	ἐν τρόμῳ πολλῷ	and	in much trembling

1.1.4. *Isolate structural signals.*

All structural signals (i.e., conjunctions, particles, relative pronouns and sometimes demonstrative pronouns) should be isolated either above or to the left, and highlighted by underlining, so that one can draw lines from (for example) the conjunction to the preceding word or word group it coordinates or subordinates.

NOTE: This is an especially important step, because many of the crucial syntactical-grammatical decisions must be made at this point. For example, is this δέ consecutive (signaling continuation) or adversative (implying antithesis)? To what does this οὖν (therefore) or γάρ (for) refer? Is it inferential (drawing a conclusion) or causal (giving a reason), and on the basis of what that has been said above? Does this ὅτι or ἵνα introduce an appositional clause (epexegesis) or an adverb clause?

Thus in 1 Cor. 2:6:

δέ		but	
λαλοῦμεν	σοφίαν	We speak	wisdom

(In a notation [see 1.1.6 below] one should note something like this: This is an adversative δέ, probably to all of 1:18–2:5, but especially to 2:4–5, where Paul has denied having spoken in words of persuasive wisdom.)

Also further in v. 6:

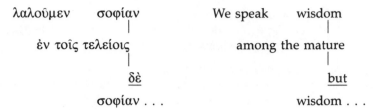

λαλοῦμεν   σοφίαν   We speak   wisdom
     | | | |
ἐν τοῖς τελείοις   among the mature
        | |
        δὲ   but
     σοφίαν . . .   wisdom . . .

Also in v. 6, note that the τῶν with καταργουμένων functions as a relative pronoun. Thus:

τῶν ἀρχόντων   of the rulers
    τοῦ αἰῶνος τούτου   of this age
    τῶν καταργουμένων   who are being set aside

1.1.5. *Color-code recurring words or motifs.*

When the entire paragraph has been thus rewritten, one might want to go back and color-code the recurring motifs in order to trace the themes or ideas crucial to the flow of the argument. Thus the final display of 1 Cor. 2:6–7 should look something like this:

δὲ

λαλοῦμεν   σοφίαν
    ἐν τοῖς τελείοις

                    δὲ

                σοφίαν
                    οὐ   τοῦ αἰῶνος τούτου
                    οὐδὲ τῶν ἀρχόντων
                                τοῦ αἰῶνος τούτου
                                τῶν καταργουμένων

    ἀλλὰ

λαλοῦμεν   σοφίαν
    ἐν μυστηρίῳ   θεοῦ
                    τὴν ἀποκεκρυμμένην
                    ἣν
                        ὁ θεὸς προώρισεν
                                πρὸ τῶν αἰώνων
                                εἰς δόξαν ἡμῶν
                    ἣν
                        οὐδεὶς   ἔγνωκεν
                        τῶν ἀρχόντων
                                τοῦ αἰῶνος τούτου

But

we speak   wisdom
    among the mature

             but

             wisdom
                 not   of this age
                 nor of the rulers
                        of this age
                        who are being set aside

    But

we speak   wisdom
    in a mystery   of God
            which had been hidden

            which
               God predetermined
                     before the ages
                   for our glory
           which
            none   knew
               of the rulers
                 of this age

NOTE: There are three motifs that should be isolated:

1. Paul and the Corinthian believers: λαλοῦμεν (we speak), ἐν τοῖς τελείοις (among the mature), λαλοῦμεν (we speak), εἰς δόξαν ἡμῶν (for our glory);

2. Those who by contrast are of this age: οὐ τοῦ αἰῶνος τούτου (not of this age), οὐδὲ τῶν ἀρχόντων, etc. (nor of the rulers, etc.), τῶν καταργουμένων (who are being set aside), οὐδεὶς ἔγνωκεν, etc. (none of the rulers, etc., knew);

3. The descriptions of the wisdom of God: σοφίαν θεοῦ (wisdom of God), ἐν μυστηρίῳ (in a mystery), τὴν ἀποκεκρυμμένην (which had been hidden), ἣν ὁ θεὸς προώρισεν πρὸ τῶν αἰώνων (which God predetermined before the ages).

1.1.6. *Trace the argument by annotation.*

The following examples are given not only to illustrate the process but also to show how such structural displays aid in the whole exegetical process.

Example 1. In the following sentence flow of Luke 2:14 one can see how the structures might be differently arranged, and how an argument from structure might help the textual decision to be made in Step 5 of the exegetical process (I.5). You will note that the NA[26] text correctly sees this verse as a piece of Semitic poetry (distinguished, you will recall, by parallelism, not necessarily by meter or rhyme), and sets it out thus:

δόξα ἐν ὑψίστοις θεῷ
καὶ ἐπὶ γῆς εἰρήνη
    ἐν ἀνθρώποις εὐδοκίας

There is a textual variation between εὐδοκίας (gen. = of good-will) and εὐδοκία (nom. = goodwill). If the original text were εὐδοκία (nominative), then one would have what might appear to be three balanced lines:

δόξα θεῷ	Glory to God
ἐν ὑψίστοις	in the highest
<u>καὶ</u>	<u>and</u>
εἰρήνη	peace
ἐπὶ γῆς	on earth
εὐδοκία	goodwill
ἐν ἀνθρώποις	among people

But a more careful analysis reveals that the poetry breaks down at a couple of points by this arrangement. First, only the δόξα line has three members to it. This is not crucial to the poetry, but the second item is crucial, i.e., the presence of καί between lines one and two, and its absence between lines two and three. However, if the original text is εὐδοκίας (genitive), good parallelism is found:

δόξα	Glory
θεῷ	to God
ἐν ὑψίστοις	in the highest
<u>καὶ</u>	<u>and</u>
εἰρήνη	peace
ἐπὶ γῆς	on earth
ἐν ἀνθρώποις	among people
εὐδοκίας	of goodwill

or:

δόξα		Glory	
	θεῷ		to God
	ἐν ὑψίστοις		in the highest
καὶ		**and**	
εἰρήνη		peace	
	ἐπὶ γῆς		on earth
	ἐν ἀνθρώποις		among people
	εὐδοκίας		of goodwill

In this case εὐδοκίας does not break the parallelism; it merely serves as an adjectival modifier of ἀνθρώποις (people): either characterized by goodwill, or favored by God (see II.3.3.1).

Example 2. Frequently key exegetical decisions are forced upon you in the process of making the sentence flow. At such times it is probably best to consult the aids right at this point (see II.3.2), and try to come to a decision, even though such matters will finally be taken up as part of Step 6 (see II.3 below). Thus in 1 Thess. 1:2–3 there are three such decisions, which have to do with the placement of the modifiers:

1. Where does one place πάντοτε (always) and περὶ πάντων ὑμῶν (for all of you)? with εὐχαριστοῦμεν (we give thanks) or μνείαν ποιούμενοι (making mention)?

2. Where does one place ἀδιαλείπτως (unceasingly)? with μνείαν ποιούμενοι (making mention) or μνημονεύοντες (remembering)? Neither of these affects the meaning too greatly, but it will affect one's translation (e.g., compare the NIV and the NRSV on the second one). But the third one is of some exegetical concern.

3. Who is ἔμπροσθεν τοῦ θεοῦ (in the presence of God)? Is Paul remembering the Thessalonians before God when he prays? Or is Jesus now in the presence of God?

Decisions like these are not always easy, but basically they must be resolved on the basis either of (*a*) Pauline usage elsewhere, or (*b*) the best sense in the present context, or (*c*) which achieves the better balance of ideas.

Thus the first two may be resolved on the basis of Paul's usage. In 2 Thess. 1:3 and 2:13 and 1 Cor. 1:4 πάντοτε unambiguously goes with a preceding form of εὐχαριστεῖν. There seems to be no good reason to think it is otherwise here. So also with ἀδιαλείπτως, which in Rom. 1:9 goes with μνείαν . . . ποιοῦμαι.

But the decision about ἔμπροσθεν τοῦ θεοῦ is not easy. In 1

Thess. 3:9 Paul says he rejoices ἔμπροσθεν τοῦ θεοῦ. This usage, plus the whole context of 1 Thess. 1:2–6, tends to give the edge to Paul as the one who is remembering them ἔμπροσθεν τοῦ θεοῦ, despite its distance from the participle it modifies.

Thus the text will be displayed as follows:

εὐχαριστοῦμεν   τῷ θεῷ
    πάντοτε
    περὶ πάντων ὑμῶν

  ποιούμενοι μνείαν
    ἀδιαλείπτως
    ἐπὶ τῶν προσευχῶν ἡμῶν

μνημονεύοντες ὑμῶν τοῦ ἔργου
      τῆς πίστεως
  καὶ τοῦ κόπου
      τῆς ἀγάπης
  καὶ τῆς ὑπομονῆς
      τῆς ἐλπίδος
        τοῦ κυρίου ἡμῶν
         Ἰησοῦ Χριστοῦ
ἔμπροσθεν τοῦ θεοῦ καὶ πατρὸς ἡμῶν

We give thanks to   God
    always
    for all of you

  making mention
    unceasingly
    in our prayers

remembering your work
      of faith
  and   labor
      of love
  and   endurance
      of hope
        in our Lord
         Jesus Christ
in the presence of our God and Father

Example 3. The following display of 1 Thess. 5:16–18 and 19–22 shows how the structure itself and the choices made at II.1.1.3 and 1.1.4 lead to a proper exegesis of the passage.

χαίρετε
    πάντοτε
προσεύχεσθε
    ἀδιαλείπτως
εὐχαριστεῖτε
    ἐν παντί

γὰρ

τοῦτο θέλημα
       θεοῦ
       ἐν Χριστῷ Ἰησοῦ
       εἰς ὑμᾶς

Rejoice
    always
pray
    without ceasing
give thanks
    in all things

for

this is the will
      of God
      in Christ Jesus
      for you

The question here is whether τοῦτο (this) refers only to the third member above or, more likely, to all three members.

It should become clear by this display that we do not here have three seriatim imperatives, but a *set* of three, all of which are God's will for the believer. That observation leads one to expect a grouping in the next series as well, which may be displayed thus:

μὴ σβέννυτε   τὸ πνεῦμα
μὴ ἐξουθενεῖτε   προφητείας

δὲ

δοκιμάζετε πάντα
    κατέχετε   τὸ καλόν
    ἀπέχεσθε
        ἀπὸ παντὸς εἴδους
            πονηροῦ

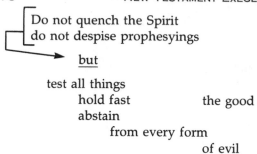

Do not quench the Spirit
do not despise prophesyings

       but

test all things
     hold fast   the good
     abstain
        from every form
           of evil

Note how crucial the adversative δέ (but) is to what follows. Note also that the last two imperatives are not coordinate with δοκιμάζετε (test), but are coordinate with each other as the two results of δοκιμάζετε.

Finally, one may wish to redo the whole in a finished form and then trace in the right margin the flow of the argument by annotation, as in the following example.

Example 4. The following display of 1 Cor. 14:1–4 shows how all the steps come together into a finished presentation of the structure of a paragraph (v. 5 has been omitted for space reasons), including the annotations:

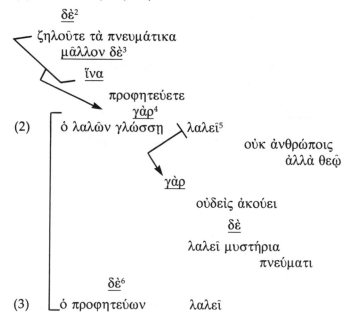

(1) διώκετε τὴν ἀγάπην[1]

     δὲ[2]

ζηλοῦτε τὰ πνευμάτικα
    μᾶλλον δὲ[3]

      ἵνα

       προφητεύετε
        γὰρ[4]
(2)   ὁ λαλῶν γλώσσῃ   λαλεῖ[5]

                    οὐκ ἀνθρώποις
                      ἀλλὰ θεῷ

       γὰρ

         οὐδεὶς ἀκούει

           δὲ

        λαλεῖ μυστήρια
              πνεύματι

      δὲ[6]
(3)   ὁ προφητεύων   λαλεῖ

                          ἀνθρώποις
                          οἰκοδομὴν
                    καὶ   παράκλησιν
                    καὶ   παραμυθίαν

(4) ⌈ ὁ λαλῶν γλώσσῃ   οἰκοδομεῖ ἑαυτόν[7]

     | δὲ

     ⌊ ὁ προφητεύων   οἰκοδομεῖ ἐκκλησίαν

(1) Pursue love[1]

     and[2]

   desire spiritual gifts

        but rather[3]

           that

              you might prophesy

                 for[4]

(2) ⌈ the one who speaks in tongues   speaks[5]
     | not to people
     | but to God
     |
     | for
     |
     | no one understands
     |
     | but
     |
     | he   speaks mysteries
     | by the Spirit
     |
     | but[6]
     |
(3) ⌊ the one who prophesies   speaks
                                             to people

                          edification
                    and exhortation
                    and consolation

(4) ⌈ the one who speaks in tongues
     | edifies himself[7]
     |
     | but
     |
     | the one who prophesies
     ⌊   edifies the church

Three themes need to be color-coded: προφητεύειν (prophesy), λαλεῖν γλώσσῃ (speak with tongues), οἰκοδομ- (edify, edification).

Notes:

1. This imperative follows hard on the heels of ch. 13.

2. The δέ here is consecutive and picks up the thrust of ch. 12 (see the repeated ζηλοῦτε from 12:31).

3. But now Paul comes to the real urgency, which is not really hinted at until now. He wants intelligible gifts in the community, and he singles out prophecy to set in contrast to tongues, which is the issue in Corinth.

4. γάρ will be explanatory here, introducing the reason why μᾶλλον δὲ ἵνα . . .

5. Paul begins with their favorite, tongues, and explains why it needs to be cooled in the community. But he clearly affirms tongues for the individual. The tongues speaker (*a*) speaks to God, and (*b*) speaks mysteries by the Spirit (cf. 14:28b). Cf. v. 4, where Paul also says that one who speaks in tongues edifies oneself.

6. But in church one needs to learn to speak for the benefit of others. (The three nouns, which are the objects of the verb, function in a purposive way and give guidelines for the validity of spiritual utterances; but the only one to be picked up in the following discussion is οἰκοδομή [building up].)

7. One more time, but now with οἰκοδομή as the key to the contrast. Note that the edifying of oneself is not a negative for Paul—except when it happens in the community.

1.2. *Make a sentence diagram.*

At times the grammar and syntax of a sentence may be so complex that one will find it convenient to resort to the traditional device of diagraming the individual sentences. The basic symbols and procedures for this are illustrated in many basic grammar books. See Harry Shaw, *Errors in English and Ways to Correct Them,* 2d ed. (New York: Barnes & Noble, 1970), pp. 383–390. This technique is particularly helpful for English exegesis and may serve to clarify the Greek text as well.

Section II.2

Establishing the Text
(See I.5)

THE FIRST KINDS OF MATERIALS from your "provisional list of exegetical difficulties" (see I.3.2) that need investigation have to do with the original text. Which of the variants found in the manuscript tradition most likely represents the actual words of the biblical author? This present section is intended to help you learn the process for making such decisions. Since this tends to be a very technical field of study, your first concern should be to understand the material well enough so that you feel comfortable with the textual discussions in the various secondary sources.

Our "hands on" concerns in this section are two: (1) to teach you how to read the apparatuses in the two basic editions of the Greek New Testament: the Nestle-Aland edition: E. Nestle, *Novum Testamentum Graece*, 26th edition (NA[26]), ed. K. Aland et al. (Stuttgart: Deutsche Bibelstiftung, 1979), and the United Bible Societies' edition: *The Greek New Testament*, 3d edition (UBS[3]), ed. K. Aland et al. (New York: United Bible Societies, 1983); and (2) to illustrate the process of making textual decisions by going through the several steps. The illustrations will be taken from the three sets of variants in John 3:15 and 13.

2.1. Learn well some basic concepts about NT textual criticism.

The discussion in this section assumes you have read carefully one of the following surveys:

Gordon D. Fee, "The Textual Criticism of the New Testament," in *The Expositor's Bible Commentary*, ed. by Frank E. Gaebelein (Grand Rapids: Zondervan Publishing House, 1979), vol. 1, pp. 419–433.

Bruce M. Metzger, *A Textual Commentary on the Greek New Testament* (New York: United Bible Societies, 1971), pp. xiii–xxxi. [JAF 113]

For a more thorough study of all the matters involved in this discipline you will want to look at one or both of the following:

Bruce M. Metzger, *The Text of the New Testament: Its Transmission, Corruption, and Restoration;* 2d ed. (New York: Oxford University Press, 1968). [JAF 94]

Kurt Aland and Barbara Aland, *Text of the New Testament: An Introduction to the Critical Editions and to the Theory and Practice of Modern Textual Criticism;* 2d ed.; trans. by E. F. Rhodes (Grand Rapids: Wm. B. Eerdmans Publishing Co., 1989).

It is not our intention here to go over all that material again. However, some basic matters need to be learned well:

2.1.1. The word *variant,* or *variation unit,* refers to those places where two or more Greek manuscripts (MSS.), or other evidence, when read side by side, have differences in wording.

2.1.2. All variants are either *accidental* (slips of eye, ear, or mind) or *deliberate* (in the sense that the copyist either consciously or unconsciously tried to "improve" the text he was copying).

2.1.3. Every variation is one of four kinds:

1. *Addition:* A scribe (copyist) added one or more words to the text he was copying. In NA[26] the siglum for "additions" is ⊤ (see p. 45* in the NA[26] Introduction). This means that the MSS. listed in the apparatus *after* this siglum have some additional words that are *not* found in the MSS. followed by NA[26] at this point.

2. *Omission:* A scribe omitted one or more words from the text he was copying. In NA[26] the sigla ° and ⌐⟍ are used for "omissions" (° for one word: ⌐⟍ for two or more). (It should be noted that it depends upon one's perspective as to whether a word is "added" or "omitted." If MS. A has a word not found in MS. B,

then either A "added" something to a text like B, or conversely B "omitted" something from a text like A.)

3. *Transposition:* A scribe altered the word order (or sometimes sentence order) from that of the text he was copying. In NA[26] the siglum for transpositions is ⌐ ⌐ (or sometimes ⌐ ⌐ when "substitution" is also involved).

4. *Substitution:* A scribe substituted a word, or words, for one or more found in the text he was copying. The siglum for this is either ⌐ (for one word) or ⌐ ⌐ (for two or more words).

2.1.4.   The *causes* of variation are many and varied. *Accidental* variations are basically the result of slips of eye, ear, or mind. *Deliberate* variations may be for a variety of reasons: harmonization, clarification, simplification, improvement of Greek style, or theology. NOTE WELL: The vast majority of "deliberate" variants were attempts to "improve" the text in some way—to make it more readable and/or understandable.

2.1.5.   The *goal* of textual criticism is to determine, if possible, which reading at any point of variation is most likely the original text, and which readings are the errors.

NOTE WELL: Not all textual variants in the NA[26] apparatus have *exegetical* significance, in the sense that the *meaning* of the text is affected in some way. The task of Step 5 in the exegetical process (I.5) is to establish the original text for *all* variation units; but only those that will affect the meaning are to be discussed in your paper, and even then one must learn to discriminate between those variants that require substantial exegetical discussion and those that may be noted only in passing. The ability to discriminate will come with experience. Some suggestions will emerge in the discussion that follows.

2.2.   *Set out each of the textual variants along with its supporting evidence.*

Although with much practice one may learn to do this simply by looking at the apparatuses, it is best at the beginning to write out these data for oneself. Let us begin with the variants in John 3:15 in the Nestle-Aland text (the text is included on p. 84 for your convenience). The first of these variants is signaled by the marks ⌐ ⌐ around ἐν αὐτῷ (in him), the second by the mark ⌐ following αὐτῷ.

For the first variation unit (ἐν αὐτῷ, etc.) you will find three basic variants listed in the apparatus, with supporting evidence. Note that

3 ἀπεκρίθη ᵀ Ἰησοῦς καὶ εἶπεν αὐτῷ· ἀμὴν ἀμὴν λέγω σοι, ἐὰν μή τις γεννηθῇ ἄνωθεν, οὐ δύναται ἰδεῖν τὴν βασιλείαν τοῦ θεοῦ.   4 λέγει πρὸς αὐτὸν °[ὁ] Νικόδημος· πῶς δύναται ⸀ἄνθρωπος γεννηθῆναι γέρων ὤν⸂; μὴ δύναται εἰς τὴν κοιλίαν τῆς μητρὸς αὐτοῦ δεύτερον εἰσελθεῖν καὶ γεννηθῆναι; 5 ἀπεκρίθη ᵀ Ἰησοῦς· ἀμὴν ἀμὴν λέγω σοι, ἐὰν μή τις ⸀γεννηθῇ ἐξ ⸀ὕδατος καὶ⸄ πνεύματος, οὐ δύναται ⸂εἰσελθεῖν εἰς⸃ τὴν βασιλείαν ⸆τοῦ θεοῦ⸄. 6 τὸ γεγεννημένον ἐκ τῆς σαρκὸς σάρξ ἐστιν, καὶ τὸ γεγεννημένον ἐκ τοῦ πνεύματος πνεῦμά ἐστιν. 7 μὴ θαυμάσῃς ὅτι εἶπόν σοι· δεῖ ὑμᾶς γεννηθῆναι ἄνωθεν. 8 τὸ πνεῦμα ὅπου θέλει πνεῖ καὶ τὴν φωνὴν αὐτοῦ ἀκούεις, ἀλλ᾽ οὐκ οἶδας πόθεν ἔρχεται καὶ ποῦ ὑπάγει· οὕτως ἐστὶν πᾶς ὁ γεγεννημένος ἐκ ᵀ τοῦ πνεύματος.   9 ἀπεκρίθη Νικόδημος καὶ εἶπεν αὐτῷ· πῶς δύναται ταῦτα γενέσθαι; 10 ἀπεκρίθη Ἰησοῦς καὶ εἶπεν αὐτῷ· σὺ εἶ ὁ διδάσκαλος τοῦ Ἰσραὴλ καὶ ταῦτα οὐ γινώσκεις; 11 ἀμὴν ἀμὴν λέγω σοι ὅτι ὃ οἴδαμεν λαλοῦμεν καὶ ὃ ἑωράκαμεν μαρτυροῦμεν, καὶ τὴν μαρτυρίαν ἡμῶν οὐ λαμβάνετε. 12 εἰ τὰ ἐπίγεια εἶπον ὑμῖν καὶ οὐ πιστεύετε, πῶς ἐὰν εἴπω ὑμῖν τὰ ἐπουράνια ⸀πιστεύσετε; 13 καὶ οὐδεὶς ἀναβέβηκεν εἰς τὸν οὐρανὸν εἰ μὴ ὁ ἐκ τοῦ οὐρανοῦ καταβάς, ὁ υἱὸς τοῦ ἀνθρώπου ᵀ.   14 Καὶ καθὼς Μωϋσῆς ὕψωσεν τὸν ὄφιν ἐν τῇ ἐρήμῳ, οὕτως ὑψωθῆναι δεῖ τὸν υἱὸν τοῦ ἀνθρώπου, 15 ἵνα πᾶς ὁ πιστεύων ⸂ἐν αὐτῷ⸃ ᵀ ἔχῃ ζωὴν αἰώνιον. 16 οὕτως γὰρ ἠγάπησεν ὁ θεὸς τὸν κόσμον, ὥστε τὸν υἱὸν ᵀ τὸν μονογενῆ ἔδωκεν, ἵνα πᾶς ὁ πιστεύων εἰς αὐτὸν μὴ ἀπόληται ἀλλ᾽ ἔχῃ ζωὴν αἰώνιον. 17 οὐ γὰρ ἀπ-

Marginal references:
Jc 1,17! · 1J 4,7!
1P 1,23 · Mt 18,3

Ez 36,25-27 1K
6.11; 12,13 Tt 3,5!
2P 1,11
1,13 R 8,5-9
1K 15,50 G 6,8

8,14; 14,17 Eccl
11,5 Sir 16,21

L 1,34

9,30 R 2,20s

32; 5,19; 8,26.38.
40; 15,15 1J 1,1-3
L 22,67! | Sap 9,16

1K 15,40!
31; 6,62; 20,17
Prv 30,4 Dt 30,
12 Bar 3,29
4Esr 4,8 Sap 18,
15s E 4,9s · 1,51!
R 10,6 · 31; 6,62
Nu 21,8s · 8,28;
12,32.34 Is 52,13 ·
36
R 5,8
18; 1,14.18 R 8,
32 H 11,17 1J 4,9 ·
5,24!

¶ 3,3 ᵀο ℵ Α Ν Δ Θ 063 f¹³ 28. 33 pm ¦ txt 𝔓⁶⁶.⁷⁵ B K LWˢ Γ Ψ 050. 083 f¹ 565. 700. 892. 1010. 1241. 1424 pm   ● 4 °𝔓⁶⁶.⁷⁵ B L N Wˢ Ψ Θ 050. 28. 1010 pm ¦ txt ℵ Α Κ Γ Δ 063 f¹.¹³ 565. 700. 892. 1241. 1424 pm | ⸂ 2 1 3 4 𝔓⁶⁶ pc j ¦ 1 3 4 2 ℵ pc ¦ ανθ. γεν. ανωθεν γερ. ων H 28 pc aur e f   ● 5 ᵀο B L N 063 f¹³ 33. 1010. 1424 al | ⸀renatus lat; Orˡᵃᵗ | ⸂vgᵐˢ; Orᵖᵗ; [Wendt cj] | ⸄ (3) ιδειν ℵ* pc aur | ⸆ των ουρανων ℵ* pc e; Hipp Orˡᵃᵗ   ● 8 ᵀ(5) του υδατος και ℵ it syˢ·ᶜ   ● 12 ⸀-ευετε 𝔓⁷⁵ 083 pc   ● 13 ᵀο ων (ος ην e) εν τω ουρανω Α(*) Θ Ψ 050. 063 f¹.¹³ 𝔐 lat sy⁽ᶜ⁾·ᵖ·ʰ boᵖᵗ; Orˡᵃᵗ Epiphᵖᵗ ¦ ο ων εκ του ου-νου 0141 pc syˢ ¦ txt 𝔓⁶⁶.⁷⁵ ℵ B LWˢ 083. 086. 0113. 33. 1010. 1241 pc co   ● 15 ⸂επ αυτω 𝔓⁶⁶ L pc ¦ εις (επ 𝔓⁶³ A) αυτον 𝔓⁶³ᵛⁱᵈ ℵ Α Θ Ψ 063. 086 f¹.¹³ 𝔐 ¦ txt 𝔓⁷⁵ B Wˢ 083. 0113 pc | ᵀ(16) μη απολυται αλλ 𝔓⁶³ Α Θ Ψ 063 f¹³ 𝔐 lat syˢ·ᵖ·ʰ boᵐˢ ¦ txt 𝔓³⁶.⁶⁶.⁷⁵ ℵ B LWˢ 083. 086. 0113 f¹ 33. 565 pc a fᶜ syᶜ co   ● 16 ᵀαυτου 𝔓⁶³ ℵ² A L Θ Ψ 063. 083. 086. 0113 f¹.¹³ 𝔐 latt sy; Did ¦ txt 𝔓⁶⁶.⁷⁵ ℵ* B Wˢ a fourth variant is to be found in parentheses—in NA[26] a parenthesis at this point in the apparatus means that the Greek word or words in the parenthesis should substitute (or, with a plus sign, should be added) for the immediately preceding word(s) and thus form another variant. You will also note that the witnesses in the parenthesis are repeated in the listing for the basic variant. This means that the editors consider P[63] and A to be supporting the variant εἰς αὐτόν; however, these two witnesses have the preposition ἐπ' rather than εἰς. For textual purposes the ἐπ' αὐτόν should be considered a fourth variant. You should also note that in NA[26] the reading of the text, when it does appear in the apparatus, is always listed as the final item. This information can be displayed as follows:

(1) ἐν αὐτῷ   P[75] B W[s] 083 0113 *pc*
    (in him)
(2) εἰς αὐτόν   ℵ Θ Ψ 063 086 *f*[1.13] 𝔐
    (into him)
(3) ἐπ' αὐτῷ   P[66] L *pc*
    (on him)
(4) ἐπ' αὐτόν   P[63vid] A
    (on him)

The supporting evidence can be interpreted by reading pp. 47*–50* and 54*–66* in the Introduction to NA[26], and by checking the manuscript information given on pp. 684–716. Thus, for example, variant 1 is supported by P[75] (a third-century papyrus), B (a fourth-century uncial), W[s] (the text supplied from another source for this fifth-century uncial), 083 (a sixth–seventh century uncial), 0113 (part of a fifth-century uncial), plus a few others. (See pp. 96–180 in the Alands' *Text* for helpful information on the various MSS.) In this way one can briefly analyze the support for each of the variants. Note that the Gothic 𝔐 listed for variant 2 includes the vast majority of the later Greek MSS. (see p. 47*).

Similarly, the second variation unit can be displayed thus. (The 16 in parentheses in this case indicates a likely assimilation to v. 16.)

(1) μὴ ἀπόληται ἀλλ'   P[63] A Θ Ψ 063 *f*[13] 𝔐 lat sy[s.p.h] bo[ms]
    (should not
    perish but)
(2) *omit*   P[36] P[66] P[75] ℵ B L W[s] 083 086 0113 *f*[1]
    33 565 *pc* a f[c] sy[c] co

In this case there are additional witnesses from the versions. For example, variant 2 is supported by Old Latin MS. "a" (fourth century) and the corrector of Old Latin MS. "f" (f itself is a sixth-century MS.), plus one of the Old Syriac (the Curetonian) and the Coptic versions (except for a MS. of the Bohairic).

For more information about further supporting witnesses, one can turn to the UBS[3]. This edition has fewer variation units in its apparatus; those that appear were chosen basically because they were judged to have exegetical significance. Thus only the first of the two units in John 3:15 appears in UBS[3]. Two things should be known about this additional evidence:

>   a. Although the UBS Greek and versional evidence is generally highly reliable, you will note that there are two conflicts with NA[26] (083 and P[63vid]). In such cases Nestle-Aland can be expected to be the more reliable apparatus.
>   b. The editors acknowledge (p. xxxvi) that the patristic evidence is not always reliable. So much is this so that one would do well to check out the church father's text for oneself before citing this evidence with any confidence.

For still further information about supporting evidence one should consult the edition by Tischendorf [JAF 122] or, if one is especially eager, that by von Soden [JAF 121]. Keys to the reading of these two apparatuses can be found in J. Harold Greenlee, *Introduction to New Testament Textual Criticism* (Grand Rapids: Wm. B. Eerdmans Publishing Co., 1964), pp. 107–113 [JAF 89].

You are now prepared to evaluate the variants on the basis of the external and internal criteria (see Metzger's *Textual Commentary*, pp. xxiv–xxxi). Before proceeding, however, it should be noted that the first variant in John 3:15 would *not* have been an easy one for a student to have resolved on his or her own. It was chosen partly for that reason—to acquaint the student with the kinds of questions that need to be asked and the kinds of decisions that need to be made.

2.3. *Evaluate each of the variants by the criteria for judging external evidence.*

These criteria are given in Metzger's *Textual Commentary*, pp. xxv–xxvi. Basically they are four:

2.3.1. *Determine the date of the witnesses favoring each variant.*
The concern here, of course, has chiefly to do with the earlier evidence—all of the cursives date from the tenth century and later. Do some of the variants have earlier supporting evidence

than others? Does one of the variants have the majority of early witnesses? Do any of the variants have *no* early support?

2.3.2. *Determine the geographical distribution of the witnesses (especially the earlier ones) favoring each variant.*

The importance of this criterion is that if a given variant has early and geographically widespread support, it is highly probable that this reading must be very early and near to the original, if not the original itself.

2.3.3. *Determine the degree of textual relatedness among the witnesses supporting each variant.*

This criterion is related to 2.3.2. Here one is trying to determine whether the witnesses for a given variant are all textually related or whether they come from a variety of textual groups. If, for example, all the witnesses for one variant are from the same text type, it is possible—highly probable in many instances—that that variant is a textual peculiarity of that family. For a partial listing of evidence by text type, see Metzger's *Textual Commentary*, pp. xxix–xxx.

2.3.4. *Determine the quality of the witnesses favoring each variant.*

This is not an easy criterion for students to work with. Indeed, some scholars would argue that it is an irrelevant, or at least subjective, criterion. Nonetheless some MSS. can be judged as superior to others by rather objective criteria—few harmonizations, fewer stylistic improvements, etc. If you wish to read further about many of the more significant witnesses and their relative quality, you should find either Metzger's or the Alands' handbooks to be helpful.

You may find it helpful at this point to rearrange the external evidence in the form of a diagram that will give you an immediate visual display of supporting witnesses by date and text type. The easiest way to do this is to draw four vertical columns on a sheet of paper for the four text types (Egyptian, Western, Caesarean, Byzantine), intersected by six horizontal lines for the centuries (2d, 3d, 4th, 5th, 6th–10th, 11th–16th). Then simply put in the external evidence in the appropriate boxes, one display for each variant.

When these criteria are applied to the first variation unit in John 3:15, variants 1 and 2 emerge as the most viable options, with variant 1 slightly favored, mostly because of the well-established high quality of P[75] and B, and because the earliest evidence for variant 2 is in the "Western" tradition, which is notorious for harmonizations (in this case to v. 16).

In the case of the second variation unit the evidence is weighted overwhelmingly in favor of the shorter reading (lacking μὴ ἀπόληται ἀλλ᾽) as the original text.

However, as important as this evidence is, it is not in itself decisive; so one needs to move on to the questions of internal evidence.

2.4. Evaluate each of the variants on the basis of the author's style and vocabulary (the criterion of intrinsic probability).

This is the most subjective of all the criteria, and therefore must be used with caution. It also has more limited applicability, because often two or more variants may conform to an author's style. Nonetheless, this is frequently a very important criterion—in several ways.

First, in a somewhat negative way the criterion of author's usage can be used to eliminate, or at least to suggest as highly suspect, one or more of the variants, thus narrowing the field of options. Second, sometimes it can be the decisive criterion when all other criteria seem to lead to a stalemate. Third, it can support other criteria when it cannot be decisive in itself.

Let us see how this criterion applies to the first variation unit in John 3:15. First, you must ask the question, which of the variants best comports with Johannine style? In this case, and often in others, you should also be aware of which of the options is better or worse Greek. There are several ways to find this out: (1) Several matters of usage can be discovered by reading Bauer's *Lexicon* (see II.4) or by checking one of the advanced grammars (see II.3.2.1). (2) The fourth volume of Moulton and Howard's *Grammar*, Nigel Turner on *Style* (II.3.2.1), has much useful information on these matters. (3) Most important, you can discover much on your own by a careful use of your concordance (see bibliographic note following II.4.3). (4) For those who use computers the ultimate tool in this regard is the software program called *Gramcord* (see bibliographic entry in IV.6).

In this case, by checking out πιστεύω (believe) in your concordance you will discover that in John's Gospel this verb takes as its object either αὐτῷ (him) or εἰς αὐτόν (into him), but never the other three options. You should also note that ἐπ' αὐτῷ or ἐπ' αὐτόν are also used by other NT writers. A look at Bauer's *Lexicon* or at one of the advanced grammars will reveal similar patterns, i.e., that πιστεύω may take as its object either αὐτῷ (him) or one of the prepositional forms εἰς αὐτόν (into him), ἐπ' αὐτῷ (on him), or ἐπ' αὐτόν (on him), but that ἐν αὐτῷ (in him) is rare.

On the basis of Johannine style, therefore, one may properly rule out ἐπ' αὐτῷ and ἐπ' αὐτόν. Those seem to be corruptions of one of the other two. But what shall we do with ἐν αὐτῷ, which ordinarily is never used as the object of πιστεύω (and never so by John), but which has the best external evidence? The answer to that must be that it is not the object of πιστεύω at all, but that it goes with the following ἔχῃ ζωὴν αἰώνιον (might have eternal life), designating the source or basis of eternal life. A check with the concordance reveals that such usage *is* Johannine, since a similar expression, in this word order, is found in 5:39 (cf. 16:33).

Thus we have with this criterion narrowed down the options to ὁ πιστεύων εἰς αὐτόν (the one who believes in him) or ἐν αὐτῷ ἔχῃ ζωὴν αἰώνιον (in him may have eternal life), both of which are Johannine.

It should be noted, finally, that this criterion is not always useful in making textual choices. For example, the words μὴ ἀπόληται ἀλλ' (should not perish but) are obviously Johannine, since they occur in v. 16. But their absence in v. 15 would be equally Johannine.

2.5. *Evaluate each of the variants by the criteria of transcriptional probability.*

These criteria have to do with the kinds of mistakes or changes copyists are most likely to have made to the text, given that one of the variants is the original. They are conveniently displayed in Metzger's *Textual Commentary*, pages xxvi–xxvii. You should note two things about them: (1) Not all of the criteria are applicable at the same time for any given unit of variation. (2) The overarching rule is this: The reading that best explains how the others came into existence is to be preferred as the original text.

By these criteria we may note that the variant ἐν αὐτῷ now emerges rather clearly as the original text in John 3:15.

First, it is the more difficult reading. That is, given the high frequency of πιστεύειν εἰς αὐτόν (to believe in him) in John, it is easy to see how a copyist would have missed the fact that ἐν αὐτῷ (in him) belongs with ἔχῃ ζωὴν αἰώνιον (might have eternal life) and, also recognizing that ὁ πιστεύων ἐν αὐτῷ was poor Greek, would have changed ἐν αὐτῷ to the more common form. The fact that ὁ πιστεύων ἐν αὐτῷ would be such poor Greek usage also explains the emergence of ἐπ' αὐτῷ and ἐπ' αὐτόν. That is, both of these are "corrections" that witness to an original text with ἐν αὐτῷ, not εἰς αὐτόν.

Conversely, there is no good explanation why a scribe would have changed εἰς αὐτόν to any of the other forms, since ὁ πιστεύων εἰς αὐτόν makes perfectly good sense and since no one seems to have made this change elsewhere in John.

Second, the variant εἰς αὐτόν can also be explained as a harmonization to v. 16. This would especially be true in those instances where the words μὴ ἀπόληται ἀλλ' were also assimilated from v. 16 so that the prepositional phrase could belong *only* with ὁ πιστεύων and was no longer available to go with ἔχῃ ζωὴν αἰώνιον. Again there seems to be no good explanation, given the firm text in v. 16, why anyone would have changed εἰς αὐτὸν ἔχῃ μὴ ἀπόληται ἀλλ' to read ἐν αὐτῷ, especially with the inherent difficulties it presents when it immediately follows πιστεύων.

But one can explain how an *author* would have done it. He did not even think of ἐν αὐτῷ as following ὁ πιστεύων. Once he had written ὁ πιστεύων (the one who believes), he moved on to emphasize that in the Son of Man the believer will have eternal life. Thus he wrote ἐν αὐτῷ following ὁ πιστεύων but never intended it to go with that verb form. But later scribes missed John's point and "corrected" the text accordingly.

You should note here how all three sets of criteria (external evidence, intrinsic probability, and transcriptional probability) have converged to give us the original text. In your exegesis paper itself, the addition of μὴ ἀπόληται ἀλλ' may be relegated to a footnote that reads something like this: "The Old Latin MSS., followed by the later majority of Greek witnesses, add μὴ ἀπόληται ἀλλ', as an assimilation to v. 16. The addition could only have happened in Greek after ἐν αὐτῷ had been changed to εἰς αὐτόν." On the other hand, you would obviously need to discuss the ἐν αὐτῷ/εἰς αὐτόν interchange in some measure because the very meaning of the text will be affected by it.

One should note finally that after much practice you can feel confidence in making your own textual choices. That is, you must not feel that the text of NA[26] is always correct and therefore is the text you must exegete.

An example might be the variation unit in John 3:13. Briefly you will note that the external evidence does favor the text of NA[26]. But at II.2.4 one must take the point of view of a second-century scribe. Which is more likely? That he had a text like NA[26] and *added* ὁ ὢν ἐν τῷ οὐρανῷ (the one who is in heaven) for christological reasons? (If so, one might further ask what could have impelled him to do so right at this point?) Or, on the other hand, that he had those words in his text, but understood v. 13 to be the words of Jesus in dialogue with Nicodemus? If so, he must have wondered: How could the One speaking to Nicodemus also have said the Son of Man was at that time ὁ ὢν ἐν τῷ οὐρανῷ (the one who is in heaven)? So he simply omitted those words from his copy. The minority of the UBS[3] committee thought the latter to be more likely. You will have to make up your own mind. But you can see from this how integral to exegesis the questions of textual criticism are.

SECTION II.3

THE ANALYSIS OF GRAMMAR
(SEE 1.6)

A SECOND KIND OF EXEGETICAL decisions that must be made for any given passage are grammatical ones (see Steps 4 and 6 in the exegetical process, outlined in Chapter I). Grammar has to do with all the basic elements for understanding the relationships of words and word groupings in a language. It consists of morphology (the systematic analysis of classes and structures of words—inflections of nouns, conjugations of verbs, etc.) and syntax (the arrangements and interrelationships of words in larger constructions). Many of the basic syntactical decisions need to have been made in constructing the sentence flow schematic (Section 1, above). This present section is designed to help you with grammatical questions that arise on the basis of morphology.

As suggested in Chapter I, you should ideally decide the grammar for everything in your passage; however, in your paper you will discuss *only* those matters that have significance for the meaning of the passage. Thus one of the problems in presenting the material in this section is, on the one hand, to highlight the need for solid grammatical analysis, but, on the other hand, not to leave the impression—as is so often done—that exegesis consists basically of deciding between grammatical options and lexical nuances. It does indeed make a difference to understanding whether Paul intended ζηλοῦτε in 1 Cor. 12:31 to be an imperative (desire earnestly) with a consecutive δέ (so now), or an indicative (you are earnestly desiring) with an adversative δέ (but). It also will make a difference in translation whether the participle ὑποτιθέμενος (pointing out) in 1 Tim. 4:6 is conditional (NIV, RSV) or attendant circumstance (REB), but in terms of Paul's *intent* the differences are so slight as not even to receive attention in most commentaries. So part of the need here is to learn to become sensitive to what has exegetical significance and what does not.

The problems are further complicated by the fact that the users of this book will have varying degrees of expertise with the Greek language. This section is written with those in mind who have had some beginning Greek and who thus feel somewhat at home with the basic elements of grammar, but who are still mystified by much of the terminology and many of the nuances. The steps suggested here, therefore, begin at an elementary level and aim at helping you use the tools, and finally work toward your being able to discriminate between what has significance and what does not.

3.1. *Display the grammatical information for the words in your text on a grammatical information sheet.*

A grammatical information sheet should have five columns: the biblical reference, the "text form" (the word as it appears in the text itself), the lexical form, the grammatical description (e.g., tense, voice, mood, person, number), and an explanation of the meaning and/or usage (e.g., subjective genitive, infinitive of indirect discourse). At the most elementary level, you may find it useful to chart every word in your text (less the article). As your Greek improves you will do a lot of this automatically while you are at exegetical Step 3 (the provisional translation; I.3.1). But you still may wish to use the grammatical information sheet—for several reasons: (1) to retain any lexical or grammatical information discovered by consulting the secondary sources; (2) to isolate those words that need some careful decision-making; (3) to serve as a checksheet at the time of writing to make sure you have included all the pertinent data; (4) to serve as a place for speculation or debate over matters of usage.

In the column "use/meaning" you should give the following information:

for nouns/pronouns: case function (e.g., dative of time, subjective genitive); also antecedent of pronoun

for finite verbs: significance of tense, voice, mood

for infinitives: type/usage (e.g., complementary, indirect discourse)

for participles: type/usage
    attributive: usage (adjective, substantive, etc.)
    supplementary: the verb it supplements
    circumstantial: temporal, causal, attendant circumstance,
        etc.
for adjectives: the word it modifies
for adverbs: the word it modifies
for conjunctions: type (coordinate, adversative, time, cause,
    etc.)
for particles: the nuance it adds to the sentence

3.2. *Become acquainted with some basic grammars and other grammatical aids.*

In order for you to do some of the "usage" matters in 3.1, as well as make some of the decisions in 3.3 and 3.4, you will need to have a good working acquaintance with the tools.

Grammatical helps may be divided roughly into three categories: (1) advanced grammars, (2) intermediate grammars, (3) other grammatical aids.

3.2.1. *Advanced (Reference) Grammars*

These grammars are those used by the scholars. They are sometimes not of much help to the student because they assume a great deal of knowledge both of grammar in general and of the Greek language in particular. But the student must become acquainted with them, not only in the hope of using them someday on a regular basis, but also because they will be referred to often in the literature.

Pride of place goes to:

Friedrich Blass and Albert Debrunner, *A Greek Grammar of the New Testament and Other Early Christian Literature;* trans. and rev. by Robert W. Funk (Chicago: University of Chicago Press, 1961). [JAF 203]

The other major grammar is:

James H. Moulton and W. F. Howard, *A Grammar of New Testament Greek* (Edinburgh: T. & T. Clark): vol. I, *Prolegomena,* by Moulton, 3d ed., 1908; vol. II, *Accidence and Word-Formation,* by Moulton and Howard, 1929; vol. III, *Syntax,* by Nigel Turner, 1963; vol. IV, *Style,* by Turner, 1976. [JAF 208]

An older reference grammar, which is often wordy and cumbersome, but which students will find useful because so much is explained, is:

> A. T. Robertson, *A Grammar of the Greek New Testament in the Light of Historical Research;* 4th ed. (Nashville: Broadman Press, 1934). [JAF 209]

3.2.2. *Intermediate Grammars*

The purpose of the intermediate grammar is to systematize and explain what the student has learned in his or her introductory grammar. Unfortunately, at the present time there is no entirely satisfactory grammar of this kind available. The longtime standard has been:

> H. E. Dana and J. R. Mantey, *A Manual Grammar of the New Testament* (New York: Macmillan Co., 1927).

This book is marred by its incompleteness, some poor examples, and use of the eight-case system, which is not followed by the better reference grammars. Therefore you may also wish to look at one or several of the following:

> James A. Brooks and Carlton L. Winbery, *Syntax of New Testament Greek* (Lanham, Md.: University Press of America, 1979).
> William D. Chamberlain, *An Exegetical Grammar of the Greek New Testament* (New York: Macmillan Co., 1961).
> Robert W. Funk, *A Beginning-Intermediate Grammar of Hellenistic Greek;* 2d ed.; 3 vols. (Missoula, Mont.: Scholars Press, 1973).
> A. T. Robertson and W. H. Davis, *A New Short Grammar of the Greek Testament;* 10th ed. (New York: Harper & Brothers, 1933; repr. Grand Rapids: Baker Book House, 1977).

Students tend to find Brooks and Winbery an especially helpful tool.

3.2.3. *Other Grammatical Aids*

The books in this category do not purport to be comprehensive grammars, but each has usefulness in its own way.

For the analysis of Greek verbs, one will find a great deal of help in:

> Ernest D. Burton, *Syntax of the Moods and Tenses in New Testament Greek;* 3d ed. (Edinburgh: T. & T. Clark, 1898; repr. Grand Rapids: Kregel Publications, 1976).

Two especially useful books that come under the category of "idiom books," offering helpful insight into any number of Greek usages, are:

> C. F. D. Moule, *An Idiom Book of New Testament Greek;* 2d ed. (Cambridge: Cambridge University Press, 1963). [JAF 207]
> Max Zerwick, *Biblical Greek Illustrated by Examples* (Rome: Biblical Institute Press, 1963). [JAF 212]

For the analysis of genitives on the basis of linguistics, rather than classical grammar, you will find an enormous amount of helpful information in:

> John Beekman and John Callow, *Translating the Word of God* (Grand Rapids: Zondervan Publishing House, 1974), pp. 249–266.

For a particularly helpful analysis of prepositions and their relation to exegesis and theology in the NT, see:

> Murray J. Harris, "Appendix: Prepositions and Theology in the Greek New Testament," in *The New International Dictionary of New Testament Theology,* ed. by Colin Brown (Grand Rapids: Zondervan Publishing House, 1978), vol. 3, pp. 1171–1215.

3.3. Isolate the words and clauses that require grammatical decisions between two or more options.

This is a step beyond 3.1, in that most words are straightforward in their respective sentences and seldom require any kind of exegetical decision based on grammar. As with other matters, such discernment is learned by much practice. Nonetheless, grammatical decisions must frequently be made. Such decisions, which will make an exegetical difference, are of five kinds.

3.3.1. Determine the "case and why" of nouns and pronouns.

The decisions here most frequently involve genitives and datives. One should regularly try to determine the usage when these two cases occur. This is especially true of genitives, because they are so often translated into English by the ambiguous "of." Notice, for example, the considerable difference in 1 Thess. 1:3 between the NRSV's "steadfastness of hope" (whatever that could possibly mean) and the NIV's more helpful "endurance inspired by hope" (cf. Rom. 12:20, "coals of fire" [KJV], with "burning coals" [NRSV, NIV]; cf. Heb. 1:3, "the word of his power" [KJV], "his word of power" [RSV], with "his powerful word" [NRSV, NIV]). On these matters you will find Brooks and Winbery helpful.

Frequently such choices considerably affect one's understanding of the text; and opinions will differ. Paul's (apparently varied) use of "the righteousness of God" (= the righteousness that God gives? or the righteousness God has in himself and his actions?) is a well-known case in point. Another example is the εἰς κρίμα τοῦ διαβόλου in 1 Tim. 3:6. Does this mean "a judgment contrived by the devil" (NEB) or "the same judgment as the devil" (NIV)?

3.3.2. Determine the tense (Aktionsart), voice, and mood of verb forms.

The examples here are legion. Is βιάζεται in Matt. 11:12 middle ("has been forcefully advancing" [NIV]) or passive ("has been subjected to violence" [NEB])? Does Paul "mean" anything by the two present imperatives (the first a prohibition) in Eph. 5:18? Does the ἀποστερεῖτε in 1 Cor. 7:5 have the force of "*stop* abusing one another (in this matter)"?

Here in particular, however, one must be careful of overexegeting. For example, in the subjunctive, imperative, and infinitive moods, the common "tense" in Greek is the aorist. Therefore, an author seldom "means" anything by such usage. Nor does that necessarily imply that using the present *does* "mean" something (e.g., πιστεύητε [that you might believe] in John 20:31). But that of course is what exegesis is all about at this point—what are the possibilities, and what most likely did the author *intend* by this usage (if anything at all)? Deciding that there is no special meaning to be found in some usages is also part of the exegetical process.

3.3.3. Decide the force or meaning of the conjunctive signals (conjunctions and particles).

Here is an area commonly overlooked by students, but one that is frequently of considerable importance in understanding a text. One of the more famous examples is the εἰ καὶ . . . μᾶλλον in 1 Cor. 7:21 (= "if indeed"? or "even if"?). In 1 Thess. 1:5, as another example, one must decide whether the ὅτι in v. 5 is causal or epexegetical (appositional)—again note the difference between NIV and NEB.

It is especially important that you do not too quickly go over the common δέ (but, now, and). Its frequency as a consecutive or resumptive connective causes one sometimes to miss its clearly— and significantly—adversative force in such passages as 1 Tim. 2:15 or 1 Thess. 5:21.

3.3.4.   *Decide the force or nuances of prepositions.*

Here especially one must avoid the frequent trap of creating a "theology of prepositions," as though a theology of the atonement could be eked out of the difference between ὑπέρ (on behalf of) and perí (concerning). But again there are times when the force of the prepositional phrases makes a considerable difference in the meaning of a whole sentence. This is especially true, for example, of the ἐν (in/by) and εἰς (into/so as to) in 1 Cor. 12:13, or the διά (through/in the circumstance of) in 1 Tim. 2:15.

3.3.5.   *Determine the relationship of circumstantial (adverbial) participles and infinitives to the sentence.*

Again, one must avoid overexegeting. Sometimes, of course, the adverbial sense of the participle is clear from the sentence and its context (e.g., the clearly concessive force of ζῶσα [even though she lives] in 1 Tim. 5:6). However, as noted earlier, although decisions here may frequently make a difference in translation, they do not always affect the meaning. The reason for this, as Robertson correctly argues (*Grammar,* p. 1124), is that the *basic* intent of such a participle is attendant circumstance. If the author's concern had been cause, condition, or concession, he had unambiguous ways of expressing that. So while it is useful to train oneself to think what nuance might be involved, one needs also to remember not to make too much of such decisions.

The question of *how* one goes about making the decisions necessary at this step is very closely related to what was said about the placement of certain modifiers in II.1.1.6 (example 2). Basically the steps are four:

a. Be aware of the options (what we have been talking about right along).
b. Consult the grammars.

c. Check out the author's usage elsewhere (here you will want to make large use of your concordance).

d. Determine which option finally makes the best sense in the present context.

3.4. *Determine which grammatical decisions need discussion in your paper.*

This step "calls for a mind with wisdom," because it will be one of the things that makes a difference between a superior and a passable paper. The clear determining factor is: Discuss only those grammatical matters that make a difference in one's understanding of the text. Some items simply do not carry the same weight as others and may be safely relegated to a footnote. But when the grammatical questions are crucial to the meaning of the whole text (as with many of the above examples); or when they make a significant difference in perspective (e.g., are the occurrences of διαβόλου [the devil] in 1 Tim. 3:6 and 7 subjective or objective?); or when they add to one's understanding of the flow of the argument as a whole (e.g., δέ and διά in 1 Tim. 2:15), then such discussion should be found in the body of the paper.

Section II.4

The Analysis of Words
(See I.7)

IN ANY PIECE OF LITERATURE words are the basic building blocks for conveying meaning. In exegesis it is especially important to remember that *words function in a context.* Therefore, although any given word may have a broad or narrow *range of meaning,* the aim of word study in exegesis is to try to understand as precisely as possible what the author was trying to convey by his use of *this* word in this context. Thus, for example, you cannot legitimately do a word study of σάρξ (flesh); you can only do a word study of σάρξ in 1 Cor. 5:5 or in 2 Cor. 5:16, and so on.

The purpose of this section is (1) to help you to learn to isolate the words that need special study, (2) to lead you through the steps of such study, and (3) to help you to use more fully and efficiently the two basic tools for NT word study. Before going through these steps, however, it is important to raise two cautions.

First, avoid the danger of becoming "derivation happy." To put it simply, to know the etymology, or root, of a word, however interesting it may be, almost *never* tells us anything about its meaning in a given context. For example, the word ἐκκλησία (church) does indeed derive from ἐκ + καλέω ("to call out"), but by the time of the NT that is *not* within its range of meanings. And in any case, NT usage had already been determined by its prior use in the LXX, where it was consistently used to translate the term "the congregation" of Israel. Therefore, it does not mean "the called-out ones" in any NT context.

Second, avoid the danger of overanalysis. It is possible to make too much of the use of specific words in a context. Biblical authors, like ourselves, did not always carefully choose all their words because they were fraught with significance. Sometimes words are chosen simply because they are already available to the author with his intended meaning. Furthermore, words are sometimes chosen for the sake of variety (e.g., John's interchange of ἀγαπάω [love] and φιλέω [love]), because of word plays, or because of alliteration or for other stylistically pleasing reasons.

Nonetheless, the proper understanding of many passages depends on a careful analysis of words. Such analysis consists of three steps.

4.1. Isolate the significant words in your passage that need special study.

To determine which are "the significant words" you may find the following guidelines helpful:

4.1.1. Make a note of those words known beforehand, or recognizable by context, to be theologically loaded. Do not necessarily assume you already know the meaning of ἐλπίς (hope), δικαιοσύνη (righteousness), ἀγάπη (love), χάρις (grace), etc. For example, what does "hope" mean in Col. 1:27, or χάρις in 2 Cor. 1:15, or δικαιοσύνη in 1 Cor. 1:30? In these cases in particular it is important to know not only the word in general but also the context of the passage in particular.

4.1.2. Note any words that will clearly make a difference in the meaning of the passage but seem to be ambiguous or unclear, such as παρθένων (virgins) in 1 Cor. 7:25–38, σκεῦος (vessel; = wife? body? sexual organ?) in 1 Thess. 4:4, διάκονος (minister/ servant/deacon) in Rom. 16:1, or the idiom γυναικὸς ἅπτεσθαι (lit., to touch a woman; = to have sexual relations) in 1 Cor. 7:1.

4.1.3. Note any words that are repeated, or that emerge as motifs in a section or paragraph, such as οἰκοδομέω (edify) in 1 Cor. 14, or ἄρχοντες (rulers) in 1 Cor. 2:6–8, or καυχάομαι (boast) in 1 Cor. 1:26–31.

4.1.4. Be alert for words that may possibly have more significance in the context than might at first appear. For example, does ἀτάκτως in 2 Thess. 3:6 mean only to be passively lazy, or does it perhaps mean to be disorderly? Does κοπιάω in Rom. 16:6 and 12 mean simply "to labor," or has it become for Paul a semitechnical term for the ministry of the gospel?

4.2. *Establish the range of meanings for a significant word in its present context.*

Basically this involves four possible areas of investigation. But *note well* that words vary, in both importance and usage, so that not all four areas will need to be investigated for every word. One must, however, be alert to the possibilities in every case. Note also, therefore, that the order in which they are investigated may vary.

4.2.1. Determine the possible usefulness of establishing the *history* of the word. This first step is "vertical." Here you are trying to establish the use of a word *prior* to its appearance in your NT document. How was the word used in the past? How far back does it go in the history of the language? Does it change meanings as it moves from the classical to the Hellenistic period? Did it have different meanings in Greco-Roman and Jewish contexts?

Most of this information is available in your Bauer-Arndt-Gingrich-Danker *Lexicon* (Bauer). In the examples that follow we will show you how to get the most possible use out of Bauer.

The next three steps are "horizontal," that is, you are trying to learn as much as you can about the meaning of your word in roughly contemporary literature, or in some of the earlier literature. You might think of these "steps" in terms of concentric circles, in which you move (in terms of NT usage) from the outermost circle of pagan literary and nonliterary texts (the papyri), to Jewish literary texts (Philo, Josephus), to Jewish biblical texts (LXX, Pseudepigrapha), to other NT usage, to other usage by the same author, to the immediate context itself.

4.2.2. Determine the range of meanings found in the Greco-Roman and Jewish world *contemporary* with the NT. What meaning(s) does it have in what different kinds of Greco-Roman *literary* texts? Do the *nonliterary* texts add any nuances not found in the literary texts? Is the word found in *Philo* or *Josephus*, and with what meaning(s)? Was it used by the LXX translators? If so, with what meaning(s)?

4.2.3. Determine whether, and how, the word is used elsewhere in the NT. If you are working on a word from a paragraph in Paul, is he the most frequent user of the word in the NT? Does it have similar or distinctive nuances when used by one or more other NT writers?

4.2.4. Determine the author's usage(s) elsewhere in his writings. What are the ranges of meaning in this author himself? Are any of his usages unique to the NT? Does he elsewhere use other words to express this or similar ideas?

4.3. *Analyze the context carefully to determine which of the range of meanings is the most likely in the passage you are exegeting.*

Are there clues in the context that help to narrow the choices? For example, does the author use it in conjunction with, or in contrast to, other words in a way similar to other contexts? Does the argument itself seem to demand one usage over against others?

A BIBLIOGRAPHIC NOTE

In order to do the work required in step 4.2, you will need to have a good understanding of several tools. It should be noted, however, that in most cases you can learn much about your word(s) by the creative use of two basic tools: a lexicon and a concordance.

For a lexicon you should use the following:

Walter Bauer, *A Greek-English Lexicon of the New Testament and Other Early Christian Literature;* 2d ed.; ed. by W. F. Arndt, F. W. Gingrich, F. W. Danker (Chicago: University of Chicago Press, 1979). [JAF 173]

If you own the first edition of Bauer, it will not be necessary to buy the second. The second has been updated in several areas, especially bibliography, but for most student or pastoral needs, the first edition is sufficient. If you have not yet purchased Bauer—and you must if you ever hope to do serious exegesis—then it is preferable to buy a new second edition rather than a used first.

For a concordance, use either of the following:

H. Bachmann and H. Slaby (eds.), *Computer-Konkordanz zum Novum Testamentum Graece von Nestle-Aland, 26. Auflage, und zum Greek New Testament*, 3rd ed. (Berlin: Walter de Gruyter, 1980).

William F. Moulton and A. S. Geden, *A Concordance to the Greek Testament According to the Texts of Westcott and Hort, Tischendorf and the English Revisers*; 5th rev. ed. by H. K. Moulton (Edinburgh: T. & T. Clark, 1978). [JAF 228]

Unfortunately, these are both expensive volumes. But one or the other should be used in exegesis, because they are true concordances (that is, they supply enough of the text for each word to help the user to see the word in its context). The *Computer-Konkordanz* is to be preferred because (1) it is based on NA[26], (2) it gives a total of NT occurrences for each word, and (3) it repeats the whole text if a word occurs more than once in a verse. Moulton-Geden, on the other hand, has the added usefulness of coding certain special uses of a word in the NT.

If you have access to a good library, you may wish to use the ultimate, but prohibitively expensive, concordance:

Kurt Aland (ed.), *Vollständige Konkordanz zum griechischen Neuen Testament*; 2 vols. (Berlin: Walter de Gruyter, 1975, 1983). [JAF 226]

This concordance gives the occurrences of a word in NA[26], as well as in the textual apparatus and the Textus Receptus. It also has coded special usages. Volume 2 gives two lists of word statistics: the number of uses for each word in each NT book, and a breakdown of the number of occurrences for each *form* of the word in the NT.

In the following examples you will have opportunity to learn how to use these, as well as five other, lexical tools.

Example 1: How to Use Bauer

In 1 Cor. 2:6–8 Paul speaks of the ἄρχοντες (rulers) of this age, who are coming to nothing (v. 6) and who crucified the Lord of glory (v. 8). The question is: To whom is Paul referring, the earthly leaders who were responsible for Christ's death or the demonic powers who are seen as ultimately responsible for it?

Let us begin our investigation by carefully working our way through Bauer (see the facsimile on p. 106). This example was chosen because it also helps you to see that Bauer is a secondary source; i.e., he is an *interpreter*, as well as a *provider*, of the data. In this instance I happen to disagree with him; but it will be equally clear that one cannot get along without him.

[NOTE FOR ENGLISH READERS: For those who do not know Greek but have learned the alphabet and can look up words, there are a couple of additional resources that will help you to get into Bauer's *Lexicon* in two easy steps:

[1. You need first to locate the Greek word that needs to be examined. There are two ways to go about this. The best way is to work from a Greek-English *Interlinear:*

J. D. Douglas (ed.), *The New Greek-English Interlinear New Testament* (Wheaton, Ill.: Tyndale House Publishers, 1990).

or you may prefer the more circuitous route (assuming the KJV) of using the coding system in:

James Strong, *Exhaustive Concordance of the Bible* (Nashville: Abingdon Press, 1980).

If you use Strong, you also cut out the next step, since the "lexical" form is what is given in his "Dictionary" section. For help in using Strong, see Cyril J. Barber, *Introduction to Theological Research* (Chicago: Moody Press, 1982), 72–75.

[2. If you use the *Interlinear,* you will need to take the second step of finding the "lexical form" of the word (i.e., the form found in the lexicon itself). To do this you should use one of the following:

Harold K. Moulton (ed.), *The Analytical Greek Lexicon Revised* (Grand Rapids: Zondervan Publishing House, 1978).
Barbara and Timothy Friberg, *Analytical Concordance of the Greek New Testament—Lexical Focus* (Grand Rapids: Baker Book House, 1981).

These two tools basically offer the same kind of help. Moulton lists *in alphabetical order* every word as it appears in the Greek NT, with the corresponding lexical form and its grammatical description. The Fribergs do the same thing, but *in the actual canonical order.* The latter is thus keyed to help you find words at the very point where you are working in the New Testament itself.

[Thus by looking up ἄρχοντες you will discover that it is the nominative plural of ἄρχων, which is the word you will look up in the lexicon.]

What follows is an attempt to take you by the hand and lead you through the entry in Bauer itself. Thus you will want continually to refer to the entry in Bauer itself, which has been included here for your convenience.

ἄρχων, οντος, ὁ (Aeschyl., Hdt. +; inscr., pap., LXX; Ep. Arist. 281; Philo, Joseph.) actually ptc. of ἄρχω, used as subst.

1. *ruler, lord, prince* of Christ ὁ ἄ. τ. βασιλέων τ. γῆς *the ruler of the kings of the earth* Rv 1: 5; οἱ ἄ. τῶν ἐθνῶν Mt 20: 25; cf. B 9: 3 (Is 1: 10); οἱ ἄ. *the rulers* Ac 4: 26 (Ps 2: 2). W. δικαστής of Moses 7: 27, 35 (Ex 2: 14).

2. gener. of those in authority (so Ioanw. in rabb.) *authorities, officials* Ro 13: 3; Tit 1: 9 v.l. For 1 Cor 2: 6–8 s. 3 below.

a. of Jewish authorities (Schürer, index; PLond. 1177, 57 [113 AD] ἀρχόντων Ἰουδαίων προσευχῆς Θηβαίων; Inscr. Rom. 1024, 21; Jos., Ant. 20, 11) of the high priest Ac 23: 5 (Ex 22: 27). Of those in charge of the synagogue (Inscr. Graec. Sic. It. 949) Mt 9: 18, 23; cf. ἄ. τῆς συναγωγῆς Lk 8: 41; Ac 14: 2 D. Of members of the Sanhedrin Lk 18: 18; 23: 13, 35; 24: 20; ἄ. τ. Ἰουδαίων (cf. Epict. 3, 7, 30 κριτὴς τῶν Ἑλλήνων) J 3: 1; cf. 7: 26, 48; 12: 42; Ac 3: 17; 4: 5, 8 (ἄρχοντες καὶ πρεσβύτεροι as 1 Macc 1: 26); 13: 27; 14: 5. τὶς τῶν ἀρχόντων τ. Φαρισαίων *a member of the Sanhedrin who was a Pharisee* Lk 14: 1. Of a judge Lk 12: 58.

b. of pagan officials (Diod. S. 18, 65, 6; cf. the indices to Dit., Syll. and Or.) Ac 16: 19; 1 Cl 60: 2, 4 (Funk); MPol 17: 2. W. ἡγούμενοι 1 Cl 61: 1. W. βασιλεῖς and ἡγούμενοι 1 Cl 32: 2.

3. esp. of evil spirits (Kephal. I p. 50, 22; 24; 51, 25 al.), whose hierarchies resembled human polit. institutions. The devil is ἄ. τ. δαιμονίων Mt 9: 34; 12: 24; Mk 3: 22; Lk 11: 15 (cf. Βεεζεβούλ.—Porphyr. [in Euseb., Pr. Ev. 4, 22, 15] names Sarapis and Hecate as τοὺς ἄρχοντας τ. πονηρῶν δαιμόνων) or ἄ. τοῦ κόσμου τούτου J 12: 31; 14: 30; 16: 11; ἄ. καιροῦ τοῦ νῦν τῆς ἀνομίας B 18: 2; ὁ ἄ. τοῦ αἰῶνος τούτου IEph 17: 1; 19: 1; IMg 1: 3; ITr 4: 2; IRo 7: 1; IPhld 6: 2. (Cf. Ascension of Isaiah 1, 3; 10, 29; Third Corinthians 3, 11 in the Acts of Paul [EHennecke, NT Apoc. II, 376] the 'prince of the world' and s. ASchlatter, D. Evglst. Joh. '30, 271f). Many would also class the ἄρχοντες τοῦ αἰῶνος τούτου 1 Cor 2: 6–8 in this category (so from Origen to H-DWendland ad loc.), but the pass. may belong under mng. 2 above (TLing, ET 68, '56/'57, 26; WTPBoyd, ibid. 68, '57/'58, 158). ὁ πονηρὸς ἄ. B 4: 13; ὁ ἄδικος ἄ. MPol 19: 2 (cf. ὁ ἄρχων τ. πλάνης Test. Sim. 2: 7, Judah 19: 4). ὁ ἄ. τῆς ἐξουσίας τοῦ ἀέρος Eph 2: 2 (s. ἀήρ, end). W. ἄγγελος as a messenger of God and representative of the spirit world (Porphyr., Ep. ad Aneb. [s. ἀρχάγγελος] c. 10) Dg 7: 2; οἱ ἄ. ὁρατοί τε καὶ ἀόρατοι *the visible and invisible rulers* ISm 6: 1. M-M. B. 1324. *

The entry begins ἄρχων, οντος, ὁ. This tells you that the word is a masculine noun (by means of the ὁ) of the third declension. Next, in parentheses, one finds several abbreviations (Aeschyl., Hdt. + ; inscr., pap., LXX; Ep.Arist. 281; Philo, Joseph.). These abbreviations, and others, are all decoded in six separate listings in the front (pp. xxvii–xxxvii). You should familiarize yourself with these lists before proceeding. The purpose of this parenthesis is to illustrate the *breadth* of usage for this word. That is, it appears as early as Aeschylus (fifth century B.C.E.), and regularly from Herodotus (fifth century B.C.E.) on (which is what the + means). It is also found in inscriptions, the papyri, the Septuagint, and three significant Hellenistic Jewish authors. This parenthesis is then followed by information as to how the word came to be formed (in this case it is the substantive use of the participle of ἄρχω).

The numbering system that follows will give the range of meanings for the word in the NT. In the case of ἄρχων you will note that there are three meanings, set off by arabic numerals. You will also note that the second usage is further divided into two subcategories.

The first entry begins with the basic, historic meaning of *ruler, lord, prince*, which is then followed by specific NT examples. It is used this way of Christ in Rev. 1:5, of "the rulers of the nations" in Matt. 20:25, which is a citation of Isa. 1:10 (and similarly used in *Barnabas* 9:3). In Acts 7:27 and 7:35 it is used of Moses, along with the word δικαστής, again reflecting OT usage.

The second entry informs us that the word was generalized to refer to anyone in a position of authority and as such became a loanword in Rabbinic literature. It is used this way by Paul in Rom. 13:3 and appears in a textual variant of Titus 1:9 (v.l. = *varia lectio*, meaning "variant reading"). At this point Bauer also includes our passage, 1 Cor. 2:6–8, but does so by indicating his own preference for meaning 3.

This second usage then is given two subentries, where it still means authorities in general, but is used of both Jewish and pagan officials. The parenthesis following "of Jewish authorities" informs you where this usage is found outside the NT. Thus one may consult the index to Schürer's *History of the Jewish People* (see II.5.2.2) for this usage, as well as specific instances found in a Greek papyrus, in an inscription, and in Josephus.

When we skip down to entry 3, we find Bauer's preference for our word. It will be of special importance here that you note two things: the *dates* of supporting evidence (see II.4.2.1 and 4.2.2), and the usage in the singular and plural. Thus Bauer begins by noting that the word is used "esp[ecially] of evil spirits . . . whose hierarchies resembled human polit[ical] institutions." Such a usage is found in Manichean manuscripts (see Kephal[aia] in the list of abbreviations on p. xxxiv) and thus is used in this way in the fourth century C.E. In the NT the devil is called the ἄρχων of the demons in the Synoptic Gospels. The next parenthesis tells you to compare the entry βεεζεβούλ (Beelzebub) for further information related to this usage. A usage from Porphyry (third century C.E.) is also given in full. In John the same usage occurs in a passage where the devil is called the ἄρχων of this world. Similar usages occur in *Barnabas* and Ignatius, as well as in scattered apocalyptic and apocryphal works (see the next parenthesis). At this point we are told that many (from Origen to the commentary by Wendland) interpret our passage as belonging here. But it is also noted that others would place it under the second listing above. Next Bauer singles out two discussions of this usage in 1 Cor. 2:6–8 found in vol. 68 of the *Expository Times*. If you take the time to consult these, you will find that Ling argues for "human authorities," while Boyd argues for both, i.e., human rulers controlled by demons, although the emphasis is clearly on the latter.

The concluding entries in Bauer give further instances in *Barnabas*, *Martyrdom of Polycarp*, and Ephesians where Satan is variously designated as the "prince" of the ethereal authority (Eph. 2:2) or the "evil prince" (*Barnabas* 4:13). Finally, Bauer gives a usage in Ignatius where in the plural ἄρχοντες refers to visible and invisible authorities; in this context invisible ἄρχοντες must refer to spiritual beings, but not necessarily malevolent ones. At the end of the entry, the letters M-M and B tell us that the word is discussed in Moulton-Milligan and Buck (see p. vii in Bauer). The asterisk informs us that all the entries in the NT and early Christian literature are included; thus the entry has also served as a concordance. (Note well: Bauer's *Lexicon* is for both the NT *and* "Early Christian Literature." The latter refers basically to all other Christian documents through the first part of the second century C.E., and it includes the "Apostolic Fathers" as well as several early Christian pseudepigraphs.)

Now let us summarize what we have learned from Bauer.

1. In the singular ἄρχων is used in the NT by both Paul and others to refer to Satan.
2. Not counting our passage, the plural ἄρχοντες is used in the NT exclusively to refer to human rulers. This includes Rom. 13:3, the only other occurrence of the plural in Paul.

3. There is no evidence cited by Bauer, either in pre-Christian or contemporary literature, for ἄρχοντες (in the plural) with the meaning "demonic rulers."
4. The first clear usage of ἄρχοντες in the plural to refer to spiritual rulers is in Ignatius' letter to the Smyrneans.
5. Scholars are divided as to what ἄρχοντες means in 1 Cor. 2:6–8.

It should be noted at this point that when the entry in Bauer is much larger than this one, it is not always easy to find the place where he discusses your passage—or to know whether indeed he does so at all. In such instances you will find ready help in:

John R. Alsop, *An Index to the Revised Bauer-Arndt-Gingrich Greek Lexicon;* 2d ed. (Grand Rapids: Zondervan Publishing House, 1981).

The Use of Other Tools

From Bauer, therefore, we have gone through all the steps in II.4.2. At this point, however, one may wish to check further the available data at II.4.2.2, contemporary usage outside the NT. The really significant data here will come from Jewish sources. Thus one may wish to consult for oneself the *Ascension of Isaiah* and *3 Corinthians* 3:11 to see that ἄρχων there refers only to Satan.

a. Here you will also want to use the concordance to the Pseudepigrapha:

Albert-Marie Denis, *Concordance Grecque des Pseudépigraphes d'Ancien Testament* (Louvain: Université Catholique de Louvain, 1987).

Because of the importance of Josephus and Philo, who use this word, it is important for you to be aware of two other tools.

b. There is a concordance to Josephus:

K. H. Rengstorf (ed.), *A Complete Concordance to Flavius Josephus;* 4 vols. (Leiden: E. J. Brill, 1973–). [JAF 455]

Here you will find that Josephus uses the word scores of times, always in reference to earthly rulers.

c. There is an index to Greek words in Philo:

G. Mayer, *Index Philoneus* (Berlin: Walter de Gruyter, 1974).

This tool is more difficult to use because it is only an index. But if one takes the time to check out the uses of ἄρχοντες in Philo, one again finds it limited to earthly rulers.

There are three other tools that you may wish to consult from time to time because they supply helpful data.

d. Since the NT uses the common Greek of the first century, it is also important to consult contemporary nonliterary usage. The chief tool for this is:

> J. H. Moulton and G. Milligan, *The Vocabulary of the Greek Testament: Illustrated from the Papyri and Other Non-Literary Sources* (London: Hodder & Stoughton, 1914–1930; repr. Grand Rapids: Wm. B. Eerdmans Publishing Co., 1974; repr. New York: Gordon Press Publications, 1977). [JAF 180]

A new "Moulton-Milligan" is in process. For the published results of these materials thus far, see:

> G. H. R. Horsely (ed.), *New Documents Illustrating Early Christianity: A Review of the Greek Inscriptions and Papyri;* 5 vols. (North Ryde, Australia: Ancient History Documentary Research Centre, Macquarie University, 1981–1989).

A look at the entry ἄρχων reveals again that only earthly rulers are referred to in these sources.

e. The lexicon for classical (and other) Greek usage is:

> H. G. Liddell and R. Scott, *A Greek-English Lexicon;* 9th ed.; rev. by H. S. Jones and R. McKenzie (Oxford: Clarendon Press, 1940). [JAF 179]

This lexicon will augment the data available in Bauer, especially in giving the history of usage and range of meanings in Greek antiquity. As we have already learned, all pre-Christian Greco-Roman usages refer to earthly rulers.

f. In many instances, and our word is one of them, it will be of some importance to trace the usage in the early church. Here you will want to consult:

> G. W. H. Lampe (ed.), *A Patristic Greek Lexicon* (Oxford: Clarendon Press, 1961–1968). [JAF 178]

In the case of ἄρχοντες it is of interest to discover how seldom the word is used of evil spirits in subsequent Christian literature. It is so used in the apocryphal *Acts of John* 1:4 and *Acts of Thomas* A.10. Otherwise the usage is limited basically to Gnostic and Manichean sources.

From the linguistic data alone, it would appear as if ἄρχοντες in 1 Cor. 2:6–8 refers to earthly rulers. It is always possible, however, that the later usage, "evil spirits," had its origin with Paul in this passage. So we must resolve the issue finally at II.4.3, i.e., by analyzing the context of 1 Corinthians 1–4, especially 2:6–16. What becomes clear in the context is that Paul is contrasting human and divine wisdom, the latter being perceived only by those who have the Spirit (2:10–14). Since the contrast in v. 14 is clearly with *human beings*, who have *not* the Spirit, and therefore see the divine wisdom as folly, there seems to be no good contextual reason of any kind to argue that the introduction to this set of contrasts (vs. 6–8) refers to other than human rulers, who as the "chief people" of this age represent those who cannot perceive the wisdom of God in the cross.

When you have finished all these steps on your own, you will be prepared to check your results with one or more of the NT theological dictionaries. Pride of place goes to:

> Gerhard Kittel and Gerhard Friedrich (eds.), *Theological Dictionary of the New Testament;* 10 vols. including index vol. (Grand Rapids: Wm. B. Eerdmans Publishing Co., 1964–1976). [JAF 252]

It is difficult to know how to guide your use of this "monumental" and "invaluable tool," as Fitzmyer describes it. Because it is so thorough in most of its discussions, you may feel as though your own work has been an attempt to reinvent the wheel. Nonetheless, it must always be remembered that this is a *secondary* source and must be read with the same critical eye as other secondary literature (see I.13). Thus, for example, in the article on ἄρχων (vol. I, pp. 488–489), Delling sees ἄρχοντες in 1 Cor. 2:6–8 as referring to the demons; however, he offers no argument for this, he simply asserts it. Therefore, by all means use "Kittel"—and buy the set if you have opportunity—but don't let it do all the thinking for you.

The other major works are:

> Colin Brown (ed.), *The New International Dictionary of New Testament Theology;* 3 vols. (Grand Rapids: Zondervan Publishing House, 1975–1978). [JAF 251]
> Horst Balz and Gerhard Schneider (eds.), *Exegetical Dictionary of the New Testament;* 3 vols. (Grand Rapids: Wm. B. Eerdmans Publishing Co., 1990–1992).

In contrast to TDNT, which arranges Greek words in alphabetical order, NIDNTT groups words according to related ideas. Thus for your word you will often need to use the index (vol. III, pp. 1233–1273). The ἄρχοντες of 1 Cor. 2:6–8 are discussed under an entry entitled "Beginning, Origin, Rule, Ruler, Originator." Again, the author (H. Bietenhard) classifies them as demons. This is a useful work, however, which compacts a lot of material into each of its articles.

On the other hand, in keeping with TDNT, the EDNT discusses all words in their alphabetical order. In contrast to TDNT, this tool includes an entry for all words that appear in the NT and gives information that is especially pertinent for exegesis.

Example 2: How to Use a Concordance

For the most part, the example just given brings you into touch with most of the steps and the necessary tools for doing word studies. We bypassed the concordance in this case because the lexicon served that purpose. Of course, a look at the concordance might also have been helpful so that you could see all the NT passages in their sentence contexts. The following brief example will further illustrate the usefulness of a concordance for word study.

In 1 Cor. 1:29 and 1:31 Paul uses καυχάομαι (boast/glory) twice, first pejoratively (God has deliberately set out to eliminate human "boasting" in his presence), then positively (it is precisely God's intent that people should "boast" in him). This contrast is not clearly available in Bauer, but a look at a concordance can be a very fruitful exercise.

First, you will discover that the word group καυχάομαι-καύχημα-καύχησις (boast, boasting) is a predominately Pauline phenomenon in the NT (55 of 59 occurrences).

Second, you should notice that the largest number of Pauline usages occur in 1 and 2 Corinthians (39 of 55) and that the vast majority of these are pejorative. ("Boasting" in human achievement, or "boasting" predicated on merely human [this age] values, seems to have been a problem in Corinth.)

Third, you may also discover that when Paul does use the word group positively, he often "boasts" in things that stand in contradiction to human "boasting" (the cross, weaknesses, sufferings).

Finally, the paradox of his "boasting" in his apostleship will also be seen to relate to the above observation, viz., that God has called him and his churches into being. Therefore, he may boast in what God does even through Paul's own weaknesses.

Thus it is possible to learn much on one's own before, or in conjunction with, consulting Bauer. Furthermore, one can readily see how important this information is to the understanding of 1 Cor. 1:26–31. Just as God has deliberately set aside human wisdom by redeeming humankind through the contradiction of the cross, so he has also set aside human wisdom by selecting such people as the Corinthian believers to constitute the new people of God. All of this, Paul says, was deliberate on God's part so as to eliminate "boasting" in human achievement—precisely the kind of "boasting" that belongs to the wisdom of this age into which the Corinthian believers have fallen. One's only ground for καύχησις in the new age is in Christ himself.

At this point you will want to return to Bauer and the other sources to determine the precise nuance of "boasting" itself.

Section II.5

Historical-Cultural Background (See I.8)

THE VERY NATURE OF SCRIPTURE demands that the exegete have some skills in investigating the historical-cultural background of NT texts. The NT, after all, does not come in the form of timeless aphorisms; every text was written in a given first-century time/space framework. Indeed the NT authors felt no need to explain what were for them and their readers common cultural assumptions. Only when provincial customs might not be understood in broader contexts are explanations given (e.g., Mark 7:3–4), but these are rare.

The problems that the modern exegete faces here are several. First, we read our ideas and customs back into the first century. So one of the difficulties lies in learning to become aware of what needs investigation. The second problem lies in how one goes about the process of investigation; and third, one must learn how to evaluate the significance of what has been discovered.

Obviously, *there are no easy answers or steps to follow here. You must make up your mind that this is the work of a lifetime.* Furthermore, this work cannot be done without access to numerous bibliographic resources, both primary and secondary. The following guidelines, therefore, are not so much attempts to guide you through a process as to broaden your perspective and to give you some suggestions as to where to look.

5.1. *Determine whether the cultural milieu of your passage is basically Jewish, or Greco-Roman, or some combination of both.*

The purpose of this guideline is to serve as a constant reminder that the cultural milieu of the first century is very complex. For the most part, the Gospel materials will reflect Jewish backgrounds. But all the Gospels in their present form have a Gentile church or the Gentile mission as their ultimate audience. One can already see some cultural shifts at work in the Gospel materials themselves (e.g., Mark's comment on the food laws in 7:19; or the topographical shift in the parable of the wise and foolish builders from the limestone hills and chalk valleys of Judea and Galilee in Matt. 7:24–27 to a topography of plains and rivers in Luke 6:47–49). Thus when Jesus speaks about almsgiving, divorce, oaths, etc., it is imperative to know Jewish culture on these points. But it would also be helpful to know the Greco-Roman culture on such matters in order to be sensitive to the similarities or differences.

Likewise with the Pauline Epistles, it is especially important to have a feeling for Paul's own essentially Jewish thought world. But because all his letters were written to basically Gentile churches situated in Greco-Roman culture, one must also look for ways to understand that culture as well.

For an overview of the political, religious, and intellectual currents of first-century Judaism and Roman Hellenism you will want to secure one of the following:

Eduard Lohse, *The New Testament Environment* (Nashville: Abingdon Press, 1976).

Everett Ferguson, *Backgrounds of Early Christianity* (Grand Rapids: Wm. B. Eerdmans Publishing Co., 1987).

For background to the interplay between Judaism and Hellenism that set the stage for the Judaism of the first century, consult:

Martin Hengel, *Judaism and Hellenism: Studies in Their Encounter in Palestine During the Early Hellenistic Period;* 2 vols. (Philadelphia: Fortress Press, 1974). [JAF 400]

5.2. *Determine the meaning and significance of persons, places, events, institutions, concepts, or customs.*

This is what most people mean when they speak of "backgrounds." They want to know how and why people did things. Indeed such information is crucial to the understanding of many texts.

The secret to this step is to have access to a wide range of secondary literature, with the special caution that one learn regularly to check the references given in this literature against the primary sources.

5.2.1. One should first of all have access to one of the multivolumed Bible dictionaries. Pride of place now goes to:

> David Noel Freedman (ed.), *The Anchor Bible Dictionary*; 6 vols. (New York: Doubleday & Co., 1992).

Although this is by far the best and most up-to-date of the Bible dictionaries, one will still find considerable usefulness either in the older standard:

> George A. Buttrick et al. (eds.), *The Interpreter's Dictionary of the Bible*; 4 vols. (Nashville: Abingdon Press, 1962); with its supplement:
> Keith Crim et al. (eds.), *The Interpreter's Dictionary of the Bible, Supplementary Volume* (Nashville: Abingdon Press, 1976). [JAF 240]

or in the recent revision of a previous older standard:

> Geoffrey W. Bromiley et al. (eds.), *The International Standard Bible Encyclopedia*; rev. ed.; 4 vols. (Grand Rapids: Wm. B. Eerdmans Publishing Co., 1979–1988).

5.2.2. Be aware of a variety of books that try to put one in touch with various aspects of first-century customs and culture. The absolutely essential work in this regard, which covers the whole NT period, both historically and sociologically, is:

> Emil Schürer, *The History of the Jewish People in the Age of Jesus Christ (175 B.C.-A.D. 135): A New English Version Revised and Edited*; ed. by Géza Vermès et al.; 3 vols. (Edinburgh: T. & T. Clark, 1973, 1979). [JAF 410]

Among others that also might be helpful, one should note:

> Joachim Jeremias, *Jerusalem in the Time of Jesus: An Investigation Into Economic and Social Conditions During the New Testament Period* (Philadelphia: Fortress Press, 1967). [JAF 534]

This work, like many others, needs to be used with some caution, since Jeremias at times disregards the date of sources (see 11.5.4.2). Another, more popular work of this kind is:

J. Duncan M. Derrett, *Jesus's Audience: The Social and Psychological Environment in Which He Worked* (New York: Seabury Press, 1973).

Among the several books that try to help one to get in touch with "Bible times," meaning manners and customs, any of the following will be useful:

Victor H. Matthews, *Manners and Customs in the Bible: An Illustrated Guide to Daily Life in Bible Times* (Peabody, Mass.: Hendrickson Publishers, 1988).

J. A. Thompson, *Handbook of Life in Bible Times* (Downers Grove, Ill.: Inter-Varsity Press, 1986).

Madeleine S. Miller and J. Lane Miller, *Harper's Encyclopedia of Bible Life;* 3d rev. ed. by Boyce M. Bennett and David H. Scott (New York: Harper & Row, 1978).

The very complexity of the Greco-Roman side (Greece, Rome, and the provinces of all kinds) makes it impossible to select adequate bibliography in a book like this. With a little work in libraries one can uncover a wealth of material, both general and very specialized, in various classical studies. A word of caution: One must be careful not to make sweeping generalizations about the whole pagan world on the basis of evidence from one part of that world.

For a useful bibliography here one is well served by:

Daniel J. Harrington, *The New Testament: A Bibliography* (Wilmington, Del.: Michael Glazier, 1985), pp. 197–200.

Two other books of a popular nature that touch on matters of everyday life are:

Max Cary and T. J. Haarhoff, *Life and Thought in the Greek and Roman World* (London: Methuen & Co., 1940).

Harold Mattingly, *The Man in the Roman Street* (New York: W. W. Norton & Co., 1966).

One should also be aware of another massive work (to be well over thirty volumes when completed) dealing with the rise and fall of the Roman world:

Hildegard Temporini and Wolfgang Haase (eds.), *Aufstieg und Niedergang der römischen Welt. Geschichte und Kultur Roms im Spiegel der neueren Forschung* (Berlin: Walter de Gruyter, 1972–).

Although this work is being published in Germany, it includes articles in several languages. Many of the articles are by English-speaking scholars, in English, and may be useful in specific areas of interest.

5.3.   *Gather parallel or counterparallel texts from Jewish or Grecc-Roman sources that may aid in understanding the cultural milieu of the author of your passage.*

This is a step beyond 5.2 in that it gets you into some of the primary sources themselves (often by way of translation, of course). The purpose of such a collection of texts varies. Sometimes, as in the divorce passages, the purpose is to expose oneself to the various options in first-century culture; sometimes, as with a passage like 1 Tim. 6:10, it is to recognize that the author is quoting a common proverb. But in each case, the point is for you to get in touch with the first-century world for yourself.

As you collect texts, be aware not only of direct parallels but also of counterparallels (antithetical ideas or customs), as well as those texts that reflect a common milieu of ideas. To get at this material you should do the following:

5.3.1.   *Be aware of the wide range of literature that makes up Jewish backgrounds.*

This material may be conveniently grouped into the following categories:

a. *The Old Testament and the Septuagint.* For editions see JAF 97–112.

b. *The Apocrypha.* For editions see JAF 104–112. Good English translations may be found in the NRSV or the GNB.

c. *The Pseudepigrapha.* The standard English translation now is:

> J. H. Charlesworth (ed.), *The Old Testament Pseudepigrapha;* 2 vols. (Garden City, N.Y.: Doubleday & Co., 1983–1985). [JAF 446]

d. *The Dead Sea Scrolls.* The standard translation is:

> André Dupont-Sommer, *The Essene Writings from Qumran* (Oxford: Basil Blackwell, 1961; repr. Gloucester, Mass: Peter Smith, 1973). [JAF 447]

For an invaluable collection of Qumran parallels (themes and subjects) to the New Testament, see:

H. Braun, *Qumran und das Neue Testament;* 2 vols. (Tübingen: J. C. B. Mohr [Paul Siebeck], 1966), vol. 2.

e. *The Hellenistic Jewish writers Philo and Josephus.* The standard editions and translations are in the Loeb Classical Library (Harvard University Press).

f. *The Rabbinic literature.* For texts and translations see Fitzmyer, pp. 126–128. The standard edition of the Mishnah is by Danby (477), the Talmud by Epstein (478), and the Midrashim by Freedman and Simon (479).

g. *The Targumic literature.* For bibliography see:

Daniel J. Harrington, *The New Testament: A Bibliography* (Wilmington, Del.: Michael Glazier, 1985), pp. 218–220.

If you are not acquainted with the date or significance of any of this literature, you should consult the two following introductions:

George W. E. Nickelsburg, *Jewish Literature Between the Bible and the Mishnah: An Historical and Literary Introduction* (Philadelphia: Fortress Press, 1981).

R. C. Musaph-Andriesse, *From Torah to Kabbalah: A Basic Introduction to the Writings of Judaism* (New York: Oxford University Press, 1982).

5.3.2. *Be aware of the range of literature that is available on the Greco-Roman side.*

The largest and best collection of these authors is the Loeb Classical Library (Harvard University Press), which has both the Greek and Latin texts, along with an English translation—in over 450 volumes.

A project that has been going on for many years, called the Corpus Hellenisticum Novi Testamenti, has been collecting and publishing both parallels and counterparallels to the NT from many of these authors. Some of the more important of these that are now available are:

Dio Chrysostom (40–112 c.e.?)

G. Mussies, *Dio Chrysostom and the New Testament: Parallels Collected* (Leiden: E. J. Brill, 1971).

Lucian (ca. 120–180 c.e.)

Hans Dieter Betz, *Lukian von Samosata und das Neue Testa-*

ment. Religionsgeschichtliche und paränetische Parallelen; Texte und Untersuchungen, 76 (Berlin: Akademie-Verlag, 1961).

Musonius Rufus (30–100 C.E.?)

P. W. van der Horst, "Musonius Rufus and the New Testament: A Contribution to the Corpus Hellenisticum," *Novum Testamentum* 16 (1974): 306–315.

Philostratus (ca. 170–245 C.E.)

G. Petzke, *Die Traditionen über Apollonius von Tyana und das Neue Testament;* Studia ad Corpus Hellenisticum Novi Testamenti, 1 (Leiden: E. J. Brill, 1970).

Plutarch (ca. 49–120 C.E.)

H. Almquist, *Plutarch und das Neue Testament: Ein Beitrag zum Corpus Hellenisticum Novi Testamenti;* Acta Seminarii Neotestamentici Upsaliensis, 15 (Uppsala: Appelbergs Boktryckeri, 1946).

Hans Dieter Betz, *Plutarch's Theological Writings and Early Christian Literature;* Studia ad Corpus Hellenisticum Novi Testamenti, 3 (Leiden: E. J. Brill, 1975).
———, *Plutarch's Ethical Writings and Early Christian Literature;* Studia ad Corpus Hellenisticum Novi Testamenti, 4 (Leiden: E. J. Brill, 1978).
——— and E. W. Smith, Jr., "Contributions to the Corpus Hellenisticum Novi Testamenti; I: Plutarch, De E apud Delphos," *Novum Testamentum* 13 (1971): 217–235.

Seneca (ca. 4 B.C.E.–65 C.E.)

J. N. Sevenster, *Paul and Seneca;* Supplements to *Novum Testamentum,* 4 (Leiden: E. J. Brill, 1961).

5.3.3. *For specific texts, use key secondary sources as the point of departure.*

Again, there are no "rules" to follow here. One of the places to begin would be with some of the better commentaries (the Hermeneia series in English, Études Bibliques in French, or the Meyer or Herder series in German). Very often, pertinent references will appear either in parentheses in the text or in notes.

For the Hellenistic side one could quickly go through the indexes to the materials in the Corpus Hellenisticum (noted at II.5.3.2).

For the Rabbinic materials there are two excellent sources:

Hermann L. Strack and Paul Billerbeck, *Kommentar zum Neuen Testament aus Talmud und Midrasch;* 6 vols. (Munich: Beck, 1922–1961). [JAF 496]

This is a collection of texts from the Rabbinic literature as they may reflect on background to the NT, arranged in NT canonical order. Although the texts are in German, an English-speaking student can collect their references and go to the English translations (for their reference abbreviations, see vol. 1, pp. vii–viii). One must use caution here (see II.5.4.2), because this collection is not always discriminating. But it is nonetheless an invaluable tool.

J. Bonsirven, *Textes Rabbiniques des deux premiers siècles chrétiens pour servir à l'intelligence du Nouveau Testament* (Rome: Biblical Institute Press, 1955). [JAF 489]

This collection is by tractate in the Talmud. However, one can use the indexes in the back to locate material for specific passages. Despite the title, not all the references date from the first two Christian centuries. Nonetheless, this also is a useful tool.

5.4. Evaluate the significance of the background data for the understanding of your text.

This is easily the most crucial step for exegesis; it is at the same time the most difficult to "teach" or to give rules for. The following guidelines, therefore, are some suggestions and cautions about the kinds of things you need to be alert to.

5.4.1. Be aware of the kind of background information with which you are dealing.

This guideline merely restates what was noted in II.5.3. Does your "background" passage offer a direct parallel to your NT passage? Is it a counterparallel or antithesis? Or does it reflect the larger cultural milieu against which your passage must be understood?

5.4.2. As much as possible, determine the date of the background information.

You must learn to develop a broad sensitivity here, for the "date" of the author of your parallel text may or may not make it irrelevant to your NT passage. For example, a writer of the second century C.E. may reflect the cultural or intellectual current of a much earlier time. Nonetheless, one must be wary, for example, of reading later Gnostic ideas back into the first century without corresponding contemporary evidence.

The problem of date is particularly acute for the Rabbinic materials. Too often in NT scholarship there has been an indiscriminate use of Talmudic materials, without a proper concern for date. Of great help here will be:

> Jacob Neusner, *The Rabbinic Traditions About the Pharisees Before 70 A.D.;* 3 vols. (Leiden: E. J. Brill, 1971). [JAF 493]

5.4.3. *Be extremely cautious about the concept of "borrowing."*

For this plague on our house Samuel Sandmel coined the term "parallelomania." NT scholarship has all too often been prone to turn "common language" into "influence," and "influence" into "borrowing." The point here is simply to raise a caution. Don't say, "Paul got this idea from . . . ," unless you have good reason to believe it and can reasonably support it. On the other hand, you can very often legitimately state: "In saying this, Paul reflects a tradition (or an idea) that can be found elsewhere in . . . "

5.4.4. *Be aware of diverse traditions in your background materials, and weigh their value for your passage accordingly.*

Does your biblical passage reflect conformity or antithesis to any of these traditions? Or does your passage reflect ambiguity? Again, one must use proper caution here. For example, 1 Tim. 2:14 says that Eve, because she was deceived, became a sinner. It is common to argue, in the light of some of the language in vs. 9–10 and 15, that this refers to a Rabbinic and apocalyptic tradition that Satan seduced Eve sexually. But there is an equally strong contemporary tradition that implies she was deceived because she was the weaker sex. Furthermore, several other sources speak of her deception without attributing it to either cause. Caution is urged in the light of such diversity.

5.4.5. *Be aware of the possibility of local peculiarities to your sources.*

This caution is especially true of Greco-Roman authors. In alluding to customs or concepts, does the author reflect what is a common, universal practice—or a local, provincial practice? Is he suggesting a norm, or an exception to what is normal? For example, when Dio Chrysostom laments the decay of the custom of veiling (*Orationes* 33.48f.), is he reflecting his own tastes, the peculiar circumstances of Tarsus, or a more universal custom?

Finally, it should be noted by way of caution that much of our background literature has come down to us by chance circumstances, and that much of our information is pieced together from a variety of extant sources that reflect but a small percentage of what was written in antiquity. While it is proper to draw conclusions from what we have, such conclusions very often need to be presented a bit more tentatively than NT scholarship is often wont to do.

But despite these cautions, this is a rich treasure of material that will usually aid the exegetical task immeasurably. Therefore, you are urged to read regularly and widely from the primary sources of antiquity. Such reading will often give you a feel for the period and will enable you to glean much in a general way, even when it does not necessarily yield immediate direct parallels.

Section II.6

The Analysis of a Pericope (See I.10 [G])

A s noted in Chapter I, the analysis of any saying or narrative in a given Gospel consists of three basic questions: (1) Selectivity—is there any significance to the fact that this saying or narrative is found in the Gospel you are exegeting? (2) Arrangement—is there any significance to its inclusion right at this point (the question of literary context)? (3) Adaptation—do any of the differences in language or word order between your Gospel and the others have significance for the meaning of your pericope in the Gospel you are exegeting?

The key to answering these questions lies in your learning to use a Gospel synopsis—on a regular basis. The steps in this section, therefore, are in two parts: 6.1 through 6.3 have to do with learning to use the synopsis itself; 6.4 through 6.7 have to do with the analysis of a pericope in the light of the three basic questions noted above, based on what one may discover through a careful following of the procedure outlined in 6.3.

6.1. Select a synopsis.

At the present time there are four synopses you need to be aware of. The following discussion will be based primarily on the first one. Since many students find the second to be useful, references to that synopsis are in brackets.

1. The most important synopsis for the serious study of the Gospels is:

Kurt Aland (ed.), *Synopsis Quattuor Evangeliorum;* 9th ed.
(Stuttgart: Deutsche Bibelstiftung, 1976). [JAF 125]

As the title indicates, this is a comprehensive synopsis of all four
Gospels. It reproduces the NA[26]/UBS[3] Greek text, with the NA[26]
textual apparatus. It also includes the full Greek text of noncanonical parallels (that is, parallels found in Jewish or Christian literature
outside the NT), and includes a full translation of the *Gospel of
Thomas.*

2. For students and pastors the above synopsis has been edited a
second time with an English translation (RSV) on the facing page:

Kurt Aland (ed.), *Synopsis of the Four Gospels: Greek-English
Edition of the Synopsis Quattuor Evangeliorum;* 3d ed. (New
York: United Bible Societies, 1979). [JAF 124]

Many of the features of the complete synopsis are kept here, except
that the apparatus is considerably condensed, the secondary parallels (other parallels within the Gospels, but found in different sequence) are not given (which is an unfortunate reduction), and the
noncanonical parallels are omitted.

3. A synopsis with a long history of usefulness (Huck-Lietzmann;
see JAF 126) has been totally revised by Heinrich Greeven:

Albert Huck, *Synopsis of the First Three Gospels;* 13th ed., rev.
by Heinrich Greeven (Tübingen: J. C. B. Mohr [Paul Sie-
beck], 1981).

This synopsis has several interesting features. First, Greeven has
produced an entirely new Greek text, which has considerable differences from NA[26]/UBS[3]. Second, the textual apparatus is limited to
two kinds of variants: those which have been regarded by other
textual critics as original and those which in some degree or other
reflect assimilation between (among) the Gospels. Third, passages
from John's Gospel are now included, but only those that are parallel to one or more of the Synoptics. Fourth, italic type is used for all
parallels that are found in a different sequence in the second or third
Gospel. Professor Greeven has also made a concerted effort to have
all parallel wordings appear in precise parallel columns and spacing;
but to do so he has allowed the lines between the Gospels to do a
considerable amount of zigzagging, which at times makes it difficult
to follow the sequence in a given Gospel.

4. A recent synopsis that is available so far only for Matthew's
Gospel is:

Reuben J. Swanson, *The Horizontal Line Synopsis of the Gospels,
Greek Edition* (Pasadena, Calif.: William Carey Library,
1984).

For certain kinds of work this will become a most useful tool. Instead
of printing the parallels in columns, Professor Swanson has printed
the parallels by lining them up across the page, one under the other.
All agreements of any of the Gospels with Matthew are underlined.
Also included is a full apparatus of textual variation, showing how
any of the major manuscripts read—also in horizontal parallels, one
under the other.

The discussion that follows will be based on the comprehensive
Aland *Synopsis Quattuor Evangeliorum.* You should at least learn
how to use this tool, even if eventually you work with one of the
others.

6.2.   *Locate your passage in the synopsis.*

After you have become familiar with your synopsis, this step will
become second nature and you will start with 6.3. But at the outset
you need to learn how to "read" the Aland *Synopsis.* The following
discussion will use the collection of sayings in Matt. 7:1–5 and Mark
4:21–25 (see the facsimile on pp. 128–129), as well as the parable in
Matt. 7:24–27, as examples. (Bracketed references are to the Greek-
English synopsis.)

There are two ways to locate these pericopes. One is to look at
Index II, pp. 576–583 [356–361], in which you are given both the
pericope number (nr. = German for "number") and the page number. Thus Matt. 7:1–5, for example, appears on page 92 [60] and
Mark 4:21–25 on page 179 [117]. The second and more common
way is to look at the references at the top of each page. In each case
you will find a reference to each of the four Gospels. These references, you will note, are in most cases a mixture of regular and bold
type. In order to understand these references, you need to understand how the synopsis has been put together.

The synopsis itself reproduces each Gospel in its own sequence
(or order) from beginning to end (that is, from Matt. 1:1 to 28:20,
etc.). Thus passages found in all three Gospels, all in the same sequence, will appear once in the synopsis. But parallel passages that
appear in different sequence in one or more of the other Gospels will
appear two or three times, depending on the number of different
sequences. The easiest way to visualize this is to familiarize yourself
with Index I, pp. 551–575 [341–355]. Here you will notice that for

each Gospel the boldface references simply follow the order of that Gospel. You will also note that the regular-type references interspersed among the bold are always out of sequence for that Gospel but are parallel to a boldface reference in at least one other Gospel. Thus at any point where both or all the Gospels have the same pericope in the same order (e.g., nos. 7, 11, 13, 14, 16, 18), the references are all in bold print and the pericope is found in the synopsis that one time. However, whenever one or more of the Gospels has a pericope reference in regular type, that means that another Gospel (or two) has this pericope in a different sequence. The synopsis will thus give that pericope twice (or more), once each in the sequence of each Gospel (see, e.g., nos. 6 and 19, 33 and 139, or 68 and 81).

Now back to the references as they appear at the top of any page. The boldface references here indicate two things: (a) "where you are" in that Gospel's sequence, and (b) that the material in that (those) Gospel(s) is found on this page. The regular-type references simply indicate "where you are" in that Gospel's sequence; i.e., it gives you the *last* pericope listed in sequence in that Gospel, but has nothing to do with the page in hand.

Thus if you are looking for Mark 4:21-25, you may open the synopsis anywhere and follow the Markan references forward or back till you find 4:21-25 in bold print on page 179 [117]. There you will see that Mark 4:21-25 and Luke 8:16-18 are boldface and that the passages are in fact reproduced on the page below. The Matthew passage referred to here (13:18-23) is not on this page, but if you look back one page you will find this reference in boldface, along with Mark and Luke. This means that Mark and Luke are in sequence for both pericopes, but that Matthew omits at this point in his Gospel what Mark includes as 4:21-25.

The little "nr. 125" in brackets in the top left corner indicates that the pericope numbered 125 in Aland's system (see his Index II) is located on this page.

On each page you will find four columns, with Greek text in one to all four of the columns, always in the canonical order of Matthew, Mark, Luke, John. John has no parallels to Mark 4:21-25, hence that column is narrow and blank. You will notice that neither Mark nor John has parallels to Matt. 7:24-27, thus the columns with text are wider here, and Mark and John both have the blank narrow columns.

A few other features need to be noted. You will notice that Matthew's column on p. 179 [117] has four different texts listed in the

Qui habet aures audiendi, audiat

125. Wer Ohren hat zu hören, der höre

»He who has Ears to Hear, Let him Hear«

Matth. 5, 15; 10, 26; 7, 2; 13, 12; 25, 29	Mark. 4, 21-25	Luk. 8, 16-18 11, 33; 12, 2; 6, 38; 19, 26	Joh.
	²¹Καὶ		
5, 15 (nr. 53, p. 77)	⌜ἔλεγεν αὐτοῖς· ⊤ μήτι ⌜ἔρχεται ὁ λύχνος⌝	¹⁶Οὐδεὶς °δὲ λύχνον ἄψας	
¹⁵Οὐδὲ καίουσιν λύχνον	°ἵνα ὑπὸ τὸν μόδιον ⌜τεθῇ	καλύπτει αὐτὸν σκεύει	
καὶ τιθέασιν αὐτὸν ὑπὸ τὸν μόδιον	ἢ ὑπὸ τὴν κλίνην⌝; ⌜¹οὐχ ἵνα ⌜²ἐπὶ τὴν	ἢ ὑποκάτω ⊤ κλίνης τίθησιν, ἀλλ᾿ ἐπὶ	3
ἀλλ᾿ ἐπὶ τὴν	λυχνίαν ⌜³τεθῇ;	⌜λυχνίας ⌜τίθησιν, ᐦᵀἵνα οἱ εἰσπορευόμενοι	
λυχνίαν, καὶ λάμπει πᾶσιν τοῖς ἐν τῇ οἰκίᾳ.		βλέπωσιν τὸ φῶς.⌝	
10, 26 (nr. 101, p. 145)	²²⌜οὐ γὰρ		6
²⁶Μὴ οὖν φοβηθῆτε αὐτούς· οὐδὲν γάρ	ἐστιν ⊤ κρυπτὸν ⌜ἐὰν μὴ ἵνα⌝ φανερωθῇ,	¹⁷⌜οὐ °γάρ	
ἐστιν κεκαλυμμένον ὃ οὐκ ἀποκαλυφθή-	ἀλλ᾿ ἵνα	ἐστιν⌝ κρυπτὸν ὃ οὐ φανερὸν γενήσεται,	
σεται, ⌜καὶ κρυπτὸν ὃ οὐ γνωσθήσεται.	οὐδὲ ἐγένετο ἀπόκρυφον,	οὐδὲ ἀπόκρυφον ⌜ὃ οὐ μὴ⌝ ⌜γνωσθῇ καὶ	9
	ἀλλ᾿ ἵνα ἔλθῃ εἰς φανερόν. ²³εἴ τις ἔχει ὦτα ἀκού-	εἰς φανερὸν ἔλθῃ.	
	ειν ἀκουέτω.		
7, 2 (nr. 68, p. 92)	²⁴Καὶ ἔλεγεν αὐτοῖς· βλέπετε τί ἀκούετε.	¹⁸βλέπετε °οὖν πῶς ἀκούετε·	12
²Ἐν ᾧ γὰρ κρίματι κρίνετε κριθήσεσθε, καὶ	ἐν ᾧ μέτρῳ μετρεῖτε μετρηθήσεται ὑμῖν		
ἐν ᾧ μέτρῳ μετρεῖτε ⌜μετρηθήσεται ὑμῖν.	ᐦκαὶ προστεθήσεται ὑμῖν⊤⌝.		

15	12 ⸀Ὅστις γὰρ ἔχει, δοθήσεται αὐτῷ καὶ περισσευθήσεται· ὅστις δὲ οὐκ ἔχει, καὶ ὃ ἔχει ἀρθήσεται ἀπ᾽ αὐτοῦ.	25 ὃς γὰρ ⸀ἔχει, δοθήσεται αὐτῷ· καὶ ὃς οὐκ ἔχει, καὶ ὃ ἔχει ἀρθήσεται ἀπ᾽ αὐτοῦ.	ὃς ἂν γὰρ ἔχῃ, δοθήσεται αὐτῷ ⸀· καὶ ὃς ἂν μὴ ἔχῃ, καὶ ὃ δοκεῖ ἔχειν ἀρθήσεται ἀπ᾽ αὐτοῦ.
			(nr. 135 8,19-21 p. 184)
18			11,33 (nr. 192, p. 275)
			33 Οὐδεὶς λύχνον ἅψας εἰς κρύπτην τίθησιν [οὐδὲ ὑπὸ τὸν μόδιον], ἀλλ᾽ ἐπὶ τὴν λυχνίαν, ἵνα οἱ εἰσπορευόμενοι τὸ φῶς βλέπωσιν.

Matth. 10: 26 ⸀neque g¹ (vg) ¦ nec k ¦ – a

Matth. 7: 2 ⸀ἀντιμετρηθήσεται Θφal it

Mark.: 21 ⸀λεγει αυτοις· μητι ο λ. καιεται W ¦ ᵀ† οτι B L 892 aeg ¦ ιδετε φ 28 ¦ txt ℵ C ℛ A D W Θ pl ¦ ⸀απτεται D it ¦ καιεται (W φ) sa bo ⁿ ᵗ ¦ ᴼ et ⸀ᵀτεθηναι ℵ* ¦ [:, H] ¦ ⸀ᵀ ᵖ] ¦ ⸀ᵀ ᵖ) αλλ W ᵖᶜ ¦ και ουχ D it ¦ ⸀² υπο B* ℵ al ¦ ⸀³ επιτ- ℛ A al ‖ 22 ⸀ουδεν W ¦ ᵀ† τι ℵ A C 0133 pm lat ¦ txt B D W Θ λ φ pm it ¦ ⸀ει μη ινα Θ λ φ ᵖᶜ ¦ αλλ ινα D W it ¦ εαν μη C ¦ ο εαν μη ℛ A al ¦ txt B ℵ ᵖᶜ ‖ 24 ᴼ D W ᵖᶜ b e l ¦ ⸀τοις ακουουσιν ℛ A Θ 0107. 0133 λ φ pm q syᵖ sa bo ᵖᵗ ¦ credentibus f ¦ txt ℵ ᵖᶜ ¦ ⸀αν εχη ℛ A Θ (0133) λ pm

Luk.: 16 ᴼΘ al ¦ ᵀτης D ¦ ᵀ ᵖ) την λ-ιαν ℵ D al ¦ λ-ιαν Θ ᵖᶜ; Cyr ¦ ⸀επιτιθ- ℛ A W pm ¦ ⸀℘⁷⁵ B ‖ 17 ⸀ουδεν a c e r¹ ¦ ⸀ᵀγαρ εστιν H] ¦ ⸀ᵖ) αλλα ινα D ¦ ⸀ο ου ℛ A W λ φ pm ¦ ⸀ᵖ) γνωσθησεται ℛ A W λ φ pm ‖ 18 ᴼ 1229 it; Mcion ¦ ᵀκαι προστεθησεται αυτω syᶜ

2sqq cf Jo 5,35; 2 Pt 1,19; Apc 18,23; 21,23; 22,5; cf 18sqq. 33 ‖ 7sqq cf 21sq. 30sqq; cf Jo 18,20; Rm 2,16; 1Cor 4,5 ‖ 10sq cf Mt 11,15; 13,9 par (= nr 122); 13,43; 25,29 app; Mc 2,16 app; Lc 12,21 app; 13,9 app; 14,35; 21,4 app; Apc 2,7.11.17 etc et Evang. Thomae copt. Append. I, 8. 21. 24. 63. 65. 96 ‖ 12(Mc/Lc)cf Mc 4,3; 7,14 ‖ 13sq cf 23sqq; cf Rm 2,1sqq; 14,4; 1Cor 4,5; 5,12; Jc 4,11; 5,9; Jo 8,7 ‖ 15sq cf 27sqq cf 27sqq. 34; cf 4 Esr 7,25 ‖ 18sqq cf 2 sqq heading (5:15; 10:26; 7:2; 13:12), with one reference in smaller type (25:29) listed underneath (the latter, which is a "secondary parallel," is not reproduced in the Greek-English synopsis). Then in the column of text itself, each of the four passages is reproduced in the sequence of its corresponding parallel to Mark. The parenthesis following each reference is to the pericope and page numbers where that text can be found in its Matthean sequence. Thus if you turn to page 77 [51], pericope no. 53, you will find Mark 4:21 in out-of-sequence parallel to Matt. 5:15.

The small numbered references under the Matthew and Luke references, found in the Greek synopsis only, are to further parallels (called secondary parallels) to one or more of these sayings found elsewhere in Matthew and Luke. You will notice that these parallels are reproduced at the bottom of the Lukan and Matthean columns (continued on p. 180). It is extremely important that you take the time to look at these references, for very often they will add significant information to your exegesis (see especially 6.4, below).

Finally, still on p. 179 [118], you should note the entry at the bottom of the Lukan column (*nr. 135 8,19–21 p. 184* [121]). This means that the next item in sequence in Luke's Gospel (8:19–21) will be found in pericope no. 135 on p. 184 [121].

6.3. *Isolate the correspondences and differences in wording between your pericope and its Synoptic parallel(s).*

This step is the key to the analytical steps that follow. Therefore, it is especially important that you take the time regularly to work out this procedure. At first you may wish to practice with copied pages. Eventually, much of the information you are looking for in the analytical steps will be discovered in the actual process of working through your pericope at this step.

The procedure itself is basically very simple and requires only two colored pens or pencils. One might use blue for triple-tradition materials and red for the double tradition (see 6.4 below). At a more sophisticated level you may wish to add three more colors, one for each Gospel as its unique linguistic/stylistic features are discovered (e.g., Mark's use of καὶ εὐθύς [and immediately] or καὶ ἔλεγεν αὐτοῖς [and he was saying to them], or Matthew's use of δικαιοσύνη [righteousness] or "kingdom of *heaven*," etc.).

The procedure is, with the use of a straightedge, to underline all verbal correspondences in the following manner (for Markan parallels):

1. Draw a *solid* line under all *identical* verbal correspondences (= identical wordings) between Mark and either one or both of the parallels (even if the words are in a different word order or are transposed to a place either earlier or later in the passage).
2. Draw a *broken* line under all verbal correspondences that have the *same words* but *different forms* (case, number, tense, voice, mood, etc.).
3. Draw a *dotted* line under either of the above where Matthew or Luke has a different word order or has transposed something earlier or later in the pericope.

By this procedure you will have isolated (*a*) the actual amount of Mark's text reproduced by Matthew and/or Luke, and (*b*) the amount and kinds of variation from Mark's text in either of the other Gospels. The steps that follow are basically an analysis of these correspondences and variations.

For the double tradition, of course, one follows the same procedure, but now one is working only with correspondences and differences between Matthew and Luke.

On the pages that follow one can see how this will appear for Mark 4:21–25 and Matt. 7:1–5 and their parallels.

6.4. *Determine the kind of tradition(s) your pericope appears in.* (See I.10.1 [G])

This is another way of putting the question of selectivity, which is ultimately a matter of determining whether such selection is in itself exegetically significant. But the first step here is to *describe* what one finds in the text, especially by determining the traditions your pericope appears in.

The materials in the Gospels are basically of five kinds (some might suggest four or three):

a. The Markan tradition, which appears in four ways: the triple tradition; Mark with Luke (= a Matthean omission); Mark with Matthew (= a Lukan omission); or Mark alone;

b. The double tradition = material that is found in Matthew and Luke but not in Mark. This is commonly known as Q, but it is less likely a single source or a single tradition than several kinds of materials available to both in common;

125. "He who has Ears to Hear, Let him Hear"

Matt. 5:15; 10:26; 7:2; 13:12	Mark 4:21-25	Luke 8:16-18
5:15 15Οὐδὲ καίουσιν λύχνον καὶ τιθέασιν αὐτὸν ὑπὸ τὸν μόδιον ἀλλ' ἐπὶ τὴν λυχνίαν, καὶ λάμπει πᾶσιν τοῖς ἐν τῇ οἰκίᾳ.	21Καὶ ἔλεγεν αὐτοῖς· μήτι ἔρχεται ὁ λύχνος ἵνα ὑπὸ τὸν μόδιον τεθῇ ἢ ὑπὸ τὴν κλίνην; οὐχ ἵνα ἐπὶ τὴν λυχνίαν τεθῇ;	16Οὐδεὶς δὲ λύχνον ἅψας καλύπτει αὐτὸν σκεύει ἢ ὑποκάτω κλίνης τίθησιν, ἀλλ' ἐπὶ λυχνίας τίθησιν, ἵνα οἱ εἰσπορευόμενοι βλέπωσιν τὸ φῶς.
10:26 26Μὴ οὖν φοβηθῆτε αὐτούς· οὐδὲν γὰρ ἐστιν κεκαλυμμένον ὃ οὐκ ἀποκαλυφθήσεται, καὶ κρυπτὸν ὃ οὐ γνωσθήσεται.	22οὐ γὰρ ἐστιν κρυπτὸν ἐὰν μὴ ἵνα φανερωθῇ, οὐδὲ ἐγένετο ἀπόκρυφον, ἀλλ' ἵνα ἔλθῃ εἰς φανερόν. 23εἴ τις ἔχει ὦτα ἀκούειν ἀκουέτω.	17οὐ γὰρ ἐστιν κρυπτὸν ὃ οὐ φανερὸν γενήσεται, οὐδὲ ἀπόκρυφον ὃ οὐ μὴ γνωσθῇ καὶ εἰς φανερὸν ἔλθῃ.
7:2 2ἐν ᾧ γὰρ κρίματι κρίνετε κριθήσεσθε, καὶ ἐν ᾧ μέτρῳ μετρεῖτε μετρηθήσεται ὑμῖν.	24Καὶ ἔλεγεν αὐτοῖς· βλέπετε τί ἀκούετε. ἐν ᾧ μέτρῳ μετρεῖτε μετρηθήσεται ὑμῖν καὶ προστεθήσεται ὑμῖν.	18βλέπετε οὖν πῶς ἀκούετε·
13:12 12Ὅστις γὰρ ἔχει, δοθήσεται αὐτῷ καὶ περισσευθήσεται· ὅστις δὲ οὐκ ἔχει, καὶ ὃ ἔχει ἀρθήσεται ἀπ' αὐτοῦ.	25ὃς γὰρ ἔχει, δοθήσεται αὐτῷ· καὶ ὃς οὐκ ἔχει, καὶ ὃ ἔχει ἀρθήσεται ἀπ' αὐτοῦ.	ὃς ἂν γὰρ ἔχῃ, δοθήσεται αὐτῷ· καὶ ὃς ἂν μὴ ἔχῃ, καὶ ὃ δοκεῖ ἔχειν ἀρθήσεται ἀπ' αὐτοῦ.

125. "He who has Ears to Hear, Let him Hear"

Matt. 5.15; 10.26; 7.2; 13.12	Mark 4.21-25	Luke 8.16-18
5.15 (*no. 53, p. 51*) 15"Nor do men light a lamp and put it under a bushel, <u>but on a stand, and it gives light to all in the house.</u>	21And he said to them, "Is a lamp brought in to be <u>put</u> under a bushel, <u>or</u> under a bed, and not on a stand?	16"No one after lighting a <u>lamp</u> covers it with a vessel, or puts it under a bed, but puts it on a stand, that those who enter may see the light.
10.26 (*no. 101, p. 94*) 26"So have no fear of them; <u>for nothing is covered that will not be revealed, or hidden that will not be known.</u>	22For there <u>is nothing hid</u>, except to be made manifest; nor is anything secret, except <u>to come to light.</u> 23If any man has ears to hear, let him hear."	17For nothing is hid that shall not be made manifest, nor anything secret that shall not be known and come to light.
7.2 (*no. 68, p. 60*) 2For with the judgment you pronounce you will be judged, and the measure you give will be the measure you get.	24And he said to them, "Take heed what you hear; the measure you give will be the measure you get, and still more will be given you.	18Take heed then how you hear;
13.12 (*no. 123, p. 115*) 12For to him who has will more be given, and he will have abundance; but <u>from him</u> <u>who has not, even what</u> <u>he has will be taken away.</u>	25For to him who has will more be given; and from him <u>who has not, even what</u> <u>he has will be taken away."</u>	for to him who has will more be given, and from him who has not, even what he thinks that he has will be taken away." (*no. 135 8.19-21 p. 121*)

68. On Judging

Matt. 7:1-5

¹Μὴ κρίνετε, ἵνα μὴ κριθῆτε· ²ἐν ᾧ γὰρ κρίματι κρίνετε κριθήσεσθε,

καὶ ἐν ᾧ μέτρῳ μετρεῖτε
μετρηθήσεται ὑμῖν.

³Τί δὲ βλέπεις τὸ κάρφος τὸ ἐν τῷ ὀφθαλμῷ τοῦ ἀδελφοῦ σου, τὴν δὲ ἐν τῷ σῷ ὀφθαλμῷ δοκὸν οὐ κατανοεῖς; ⁴ἢ πῶς ἐρεῖς τῷ ἀδελφῷ σου· Ἄφες ἐκβάλω τὸ κάρφος ἐκ τοῦ ὀφθαλμοῦ σου, καὶ ἰδοὺ ἡ δοκὸς ἐν τῷ ὀφθαλμῷ σοῦ; ⁵ὑποκριτά, ἔκβαλε πρῶτον ἐκ τοῦ ὀφθαλμοῦ σοῦ τὴν δοκόν, καὶ τότε διαβλέψεις ἐκβαλεῖν τὸ κάρφος ἐκ τοῦ ὀφθαλμοῦ τοῦ ἀδελφοῦ σου.

Luke 6:37-42

³⁷Καὶ μὴ κρίνετε, καὶ οὐ μὴ κριθῆτε· καὶ μὴ καταδικάζετε, καὶ οὐ μὴ καταδικασθῆτε. ἀπολύετε, καὶ ἀπολυθήσεσθε· ³⁸δίδοτε, καὶ δοθήσεται ὑμῖν· μέτρον καλὸν πεπιεσμένον σεσαλευμένον ὑπερεκχυννόμενον δώσουσιν εἰς τὸν κόλπον ὑμῶν· ᾧ γὰρ μέτρῳ μετρεῖτε ἀντιμετρηθήσεται ὑμῖν. ³⁹Εἶπεν δὲ καὶ παραβολὴν αὐτοῖς· Μήτι δύναται τυφλὸς τυφλὸν ὁδηγεῖν; οὐχὶ ἀμφότεροι εἰς βόθυνον ἐμπεσοῦνται; ⁴⁰οὐκ ἔστιν μαθητὴς ὑπὲρ τὸν διδάσκαλον· κατηρτισμένος δὲ πᾶς ἔσται ὡς ὁ διδάσκαλος αὐτοῦ. ⁴¹Τί δὲ βλέπεις τὸ κάρφος τὸ ἐν τῷ ὀφθαλμῷ τοῦ ἀδελφοῦ σου, τὴν δὲ δοκὸν τὴν ἐν τῷ ἰδίῳ ὀφθαλμῷ οὐ κατανοεῖς; ⁴²πῶς δύνασαι λέγειν τῷ ἀδελφῷ σου· Ἀδελφέ, ἄφες ἐκβάλω τὸ κάρφος τὸ ἐν τῷ ὀφθαλμῷ σου, αὐτὸς τὴν ἐν τῷ ὀφθαλμῷ σοῦ δοκὸν οὐ βλέπων; ὑποκριτά, ἔκβαλε πρῶτον τὴν δοκὸν ἐκ τοῦ ὀφθαλμοῦ σου, καὶ τότε διαβλέψεις τὸ κάρφος τὸ ἐν τῷ ὀφθαλμῷ τοῦ ἀδελφοῦ σου ἐκβαλεῖν.

68. On Judging (RSV)

Matt. 7:1-5

1 "Judge not, that you be not judged. 2 For with the judgment you pronounce you will be judged,

and the measure you give will be the

measure you get.

3 Why do you see the speck that is in your brother's eye, but do not notice the log that is in your own eye? 4 Or how can you say to your brother, 'Let me take the speck out   of your eye,' when there is   the log   in your own eye? 5 You hypocrite, first take the log out of your own eye, and then you will see clearly to take   the speck out of your brother's eye.

Luke 6:37-42

                                              condemn not, and 37 "Judge not, and you will not be judged;

you will not be condemned; forgive, and you will be forgiven; 38 give, and it will be given to you; good measure, pressed down, shaken together, running over, will be put into your lap. For the measure you give will be the measure you get back."39 He also told them a parable: "Can a blind man lead a blind man? Will they not both fall into a pit? 40 A disciple is not above his teacher, but every one when he is fully taught will be like his teacher. 41 Why do you see the speck that is in your brother's eye, but do not notice the log that is in your own eye? 42 Or how can you say to your brother, 'Brother, let me take out the speck that is in your eye,' when you yourself do not see the log that is in your own eye? You hypocrite, first take the log out of your own eye, and then you will see clearly to take out the speck that is in your brother's eye.

   c. The Matthean tradition = material peculiar to Matthew,
      some of which of course could have belonged to Q but
      was omitted by Luke;
   d. The Lukan tradition = material peculiar to Luke; and
   e. The Johannine tradition = material peculiar to John.

It should be noted furthermore that occasionally there is an over-
lap between the Markan and double traditions, which in part ac-
counts for some of the agreements of Matthew and Luke against
Mark as well as for some of the doublets in Matthew and Luke.

For the most part "determining the tradition" is simply a matter
of noting to which of these five your pericope belongs. However,
sometimes for Matthew and Luke this becomes a bit more complex,
precisely because one must determine whether the "parallel" with
Mark is following Mark or belongs to Q. For example, in pericope
no. 125 (Mark 4:21–25 and parallels [see pp. 132–133]) Mark has a
collection of five different sayings (we will note at II.6.5 how this
may be determined), conveniently set out in this instance by the
verse division. You will note that Luke alone is following Mark's
sequence here, and that he reproduces three of the sayings, plus the
"take heed therefore how you hear" from v. 24. You might also note
from the underlining in step 6.3 that he reproduces vs. 22 and 25
much more closely than he does v. 21.

You should note that Matthew has four of the five sayings, but all
at different places in his Gospel. However, it should also be recognized that his wording is very little like Mark's in the first two instances but very close to Mark in the last. By looking at the
"secondary" parallels in Luke's column, one can now make some
judgments about the Matthean parallels, as well as about Luke 8:16
(the verse in Luke that is less like Mark). If you were to red-underline
Matt. 10:26 in parallel with Luke 12:2 (see pericope no. 101, where
10:26 appears in its Matthean sequence, for the reasons for doing
this), you will discover that Matt. 10:26 is not a true parallel to Mark
4:22 but is a Q version of the same saying. Similarly, a comparison of
Matt. 5:15 with Luke 11:33 suggests that there is a Q version of this
saying as well (see pericope no. 192, p. 275 [175]), and that Luke,
even when following Mark, tends to prefer that version—although
the Markan parallel has supplied the imagery of "placing the lamp
under a bed."

Thus one may reasonably conclude about this pericope (1) that
Luke has generally reproduced Mark, but omits two short sayings
and rewrites the first under the influence of another version of it;

and (2) that Matthew omits the whole lot, except for v. 25, which he has inserted a few verses earlier in the "reason for speaking in parables" (as a further explanation of why the disciples have been given to know the mysteries of the kingdom).

The question of the *significance* of selectivity will vary from Gospel writer to Gospel writer. For John's Gospel one should take seriously the author's summary remark that everything is included to meet the aim stated in 20:30–31. The recurring question, then, should always be: How does this narrative fit into John's purpose of demonstrating Jesus to be Messiah and Son of God?

For Mark's Gospel one may also assume that the inclusion of a saying or pericope has significance. This is especially true if it also can be shown to fit his arrangement (step 6.5). But one must also be open to the possibility that some things are included simply because they were available to him.

For Matthew and Luke inclusion of something from Mark may or may not be significant. Nonetheless, the fact that they both at times choose *not* to include something and that they generally adapt what they do include suggests that selectivity has significance. For the double and single tradition, of course, the question is the same as for Mark and John: Is the inclusion of this saying or narrative related to the known special interests of the Evangelist? In most instances the answer is clearly yes.

6.5. *Analyze the sequence of the pericope in the Gospel you are exegeting.* (See 1.10.2 [G])

This part of the analysis has to do with the Gospel writer's *arrangement* of his materials, and therefore has to do with the question of *literary context*. It asks the question, Why is it included *here*, in *this* sequence?

6.5.1. *The Gospel of Mark*

The clues to the significance of arrangement for Mark are most often internal. That is, one simply has to read and reread a large section of text and ask over and again, Why has Mark included this here? In many instances that will become very clear as you read. For example, the collection of narratives in Mark 1:21–44 has one clear motif throughout: Jesus' mighty deeds, which generated great enthusiasm and popularity, so that he could no longer "enter a town openly" (v. 45).

Likewise, the collection of conflict stories in Mark 2:1–3:6, with their recurrent theme of "Why?" (2:7, 16, 18, 24) and conclusion in 3:6 of the entrenchment of enmity, has its own easily discernible clues.

Sometimes this help comes from the exercise at step 6.3 above (through the underlinings). As one observes what Matthew or Luke does with Mark's account, that often highlights Mark's own arrangement. This would especially be true of Mark 4:21–25, noted above. There are two things that suggest that this is a Markan arrangement: (1) the fact that most of the sayings exist independently of this arrangement in the double tradition; (2) the use of καὶ ἔλεγεν αὐτοῖς, which Mark frequently uses to attach an additional saying to a pericope (see Mark 4:21 and 24, where this phrase stands out in Mark because it is not underlined).

Given that this is a Markan arrangement and that it appears in a section on parables and the mystery of the kingdom, which is "given" to the disciples but not to those outside, then one's exegesis here must ask how these sayings are to be understood in this *context*.

6.5.2. *The Gospels of Matthew and Luke*

The question of sequence, or literary context, for these Gospels depends on whether the pericope comes from Mark or belongs to the double or single tradition. If their sequence is the same as Mark's, that ordinarily simply means they are following his order. Usually *their* unique presentation of such material will be found at step 6.6, below. However, when they *differ* from Mark's sequence, then one may argue that they have good reason to do so and exegesis must include seeking that reason (see the illustration in 6.6.1b).

For the double or single tradition, one must ask questions similar to those for Mark's Gospel above. For the double tradition, however, it is almost always relevant to note carefully where and how the other Gospel writer places the same pericope. Note especially the pericopes in Matt. 7:1–5 ‖ Luke 6:37–42. You will observe that Luke has two major insertions into material that is otherwise verbally very close to Matthew. In Matthew's sequence, which very likely belongs to Q, the whole collection is instruction on not judging a brother. In Luke's sequence, however, there are now two packages of teaching, one on "response in kind," with both negative and positive items, and one that is a little more difficult to apprehend, but that seems to point to one's need to be taught as grounds for not judging a brother or sister.

Similarly with the single tradition in Matthew or Luke, the

ability to see the Evangelist's interest in arrangement is usually related to analyzing where he has inserted it into the Markan framework.

6.5.3. *The Gospel of John*

Here the question of arrangement is similar to that of Mark, but is in this case especially related to one's overall understanding of the Johannine structure. If the Jewish feasts are the clues to understanding the material in John 2:12–12:50, as many think, then this becomes something of a clue to the questions of literary context. In any case, John's independence of the Synoptic tradition (for the most part) means that clues of arrangement are basically internal—although the placement of some things that he has in common with the Synoptics (e.g., the cleansing of the Temple, the anointing at Bethany) do offer some help in seeing the Johannine perspective.

6.6. *Determine whether your Evangelist's adaptation of the pericope is significant for your interpretation of the text.* (See I.10.3 [G])

The key to this step is to go back to 6.3, above, and analyze carefully the differences between (among) the Gospels. Such an analysis should be looking for four things: (1) rearrangements of material (step 6.5), (2) additions or omissions of material, (3) stylistic changes, (4) actual differences in wording. A combination of these items will usually lead you to a fairly accurate appraisal of the author's interests. But NOTE WELL: You must learn to distinguish between your *description* of what an author has done, which should be somewhat objective, and your *interpretation* as to *why* he has done it, which can become rather subjective. While it is true that the task of interpretation here is indeed to discover the author's *intent*, one must exercise proper caution against a full identification of one's own discoveries with that actual intent.

6.6.1. *The Triple Tradition* (Mark-Matthew-Luke)

a. *Mark*. Because Mark was almost certainly working with primarily oral materials, which we in turn must reconstruct from his Gospel, there is always a certain amount of speculation about his adaptation of the material. It is much easier to see his hand at work in the arranging process. Nonetheless, certain linguistic and stylistic features of his Gospel have been isolated as clearly Markan. On this matter you will find much help in:

> E. J. Pryke, *Redactional Style in the Marcan Gospel;* SNTS Monograph Series, 33 (Cambridge: Cambridge University Press, 1978).

b. *Matthew and Luke.* Here one is on much firmer ground because of their use of Mark. In this case we will illustrate the whole process by looking at Luke's redaction of Mark in Luke 8:16–18 ‖ Mark 4:21–25.

First it must be emphasized that such an analysis must look at the larger unit (Luke 8:4–21) and see how vs. 16–18 fit in. Between a careful look at Index I in your synopsis (pp. 558–559 [345–346]) and a careful analysis of your blue underlinings, the following descriptive observations can be made (NOTE WELL: In order to make sense of what follows, you will need to keep your synopsis handy!):

1. Luke has last followed Mark at Luke 6:12–16 (Mark 3:13–19). He has in the meantime included a large block of non-Markan material (Luke 6:17–7:50). When he returns to Mark, he omits Mark 3:20–21 (where Jesus' family go to rescue him because many people think he is mad), follows Q versions of Mark 3:22–27 and 28–30 and inserts them at different places in his Gospel, and finally inverts the order of Mark 3:31–35 by placing it at the conclusion of this section (Luke 8:4–21) having to do with teaching in parables. At the end of the section he also omits Mark 4:26–34.

2. Luke introduces the section (8:1–3) by noting that Jesus is again involved in an itinerant ministry of preaching, accompanied by the Twelve and several women.

3. In Luke 8:4 the context for the parable of the sower is not the sea with Jesus in a boat (thus in 8:22 Luke must adapt by having Jesus "one day" getting into a boat), but "people from town after town" coming to him.

4. In the parable itself (Luke 8:5–8) there are several interesting adaptations: (*a*) the addition of "his seed" (v. 5); (*b*) the addition of "was trodden under foot" (v. 5); (*c*) the change from "no root" to "no moisture" in v. 6, with the omission of "no depth of soil" and the scorching sun; (*d*) the omission of "it yielded no grain" (v. 7); (*e*) in v. 8 the omission of "growing up and increasing" and the limiting of the yield to a hundredfold. The net result is a

condensed version of Mark's parable, with many of the details omitted.

5. In the section on the reason for speaking in parables (Luke 8:9–10 ‖ Mark 4:10–12), Luke omits the reference to their being alone, changes the disciples' question to refer to *this* parable in particular, changes "the mystery" of the kingdom to "the mysteries," changes "those outside" to "the rest," and considerably abbreviates the quotation from Isaiah.

6. In the interpretation of the parable (Luke 8:11–15) the emphasis shifts from the sower to the seed, which is "the word of God," and its effects on people. Thus the first have the word taken away by the devil, lest "they believe and be saved." The second group "believe" (instead of "endure") for a while and fall away in a time of "temptation" (instead of "tribulation or persecution on account of the word"). The third hear, but their fruit "does not mature," while the fourth are those who hear the word, "hold it fast with a noble and good heart and bear fruit with patience."

7. In our section of interest (Luke 8:16–18), Luke (*a*) omits the two occurrences of καὶ ἔλεγεν αὐτοῖς (and he was saying to them), thus linking v. 16 directly to the interpretation of the parable of the sown seed; (*b*) uses the Q version of the first saying, which is interested in the fact that those who enter will see the light; (*c*) in v. 17 adds "that shall not be known"; (*d*) omits Mark 4:24b altogether so that v. 25 in Mark is joined directly, as an explanation, to "take heed then how you hear."

8. Finally, Mark 3:31–35 has been rearranged to serve as a conclusion to this section (Luke 8:19–21), and considerably adapted so that emphasis is on the final pronouncement: "My mother and my brothers are those who *hear the word of God and do it.*"

If you have followed this collection of observations *in your synopsis*, the results should have become clear: The section as a whole, which begins with Jesus' itinerant preaching and "evangelizing" about the kingdom of God, is concerned with him as a teacher of the word of God and with how people hear the word. Precisely how vs. 16–18 fit into that scheme may not be quite so clear, but it is certainly arguable that Luke's concern here is with the future ministry of the disciples, who had the parables explained to them, and who were to "bear fruit with patience," by taking what was "hidden" and making it known so that people might "see the light."

Note again that the task of exegesis at this point is first of all to *describe* what the author did, and then to offer an *interpretation* of the intent.

6.6.2. *The Double Tradition* (Matthew-Luke)

Here the descriptive concerns are threefold:

1. Since almost none of these materials is in the same sequence in the two Gospels, begin with a description of the larger section into which each Evangelist has fitted the saying.

2. Determine by an analysis of the linguistic correspondences whether the two authors had access to a common source (most highly probable with Matt. 7:1–5 ‖ Luke 6:37–42) or whether they reflect two different traditions of the same pericope (e.g., Matt. 25:14–30 ‖ Luke 19:11–27, parable of the talents/pounds).

3. By an analysis of Matthean and Lukan linguistic and stylistic habits, try to determine which Evangelist has the more primitive expression of the saying and how each has adapted it to his interests.

Thus by careful analysis of the parable of the wise and foolish builders, one can show that much of the noncommon language in Luke's version is unique to him in the NT. Furthermore, the differences between digging deep and laying a foundation on rock (Luke) and building on the rock (Matthew), between a flood arising (Luke) and rains causing the flooding (Matthew), and between building on the ground with no foundation (Luke) and building on "sand" (Matthew) reflect the differences between Jesus' own native Palestine, with its limestone hills and chalk valleys, and Luke's (or his readers') more common experience of floods by rising rivers.

In this case, however, the parable, which seems most likely already to have been at the conclusion of a prior collection of sayings (much like Luke's version), functions in a similar way for both Evangelists. For a considerably different perspective, based on arrangement and adaptation, try doing this for yourself with the parable of the lost/straying sheep (Matt. 18:10–14 ‖ Luke 15:3–7).

6.7. *Rethink the location of your pericope in its present literary context in your Gospel.*

This final step is but to repeat a part of the descriptive process outlined above. It needs to be repeated as a final word, because there is always the great danger that one may analyze a saying or pericope in great detail but lose its function in the overall literary context of the author. The Evangelists, after all, did *not intend* us to read their Gospels side by side, but to read each as a document with its own literary integrity. Thus, although for interpreting purposes you must learn to go through the steps outlined in this section, you must also remember that the Gospels come to us in canonical order and finally are to be understood as wholes, one following the other.

III

Short Guide
for Sermon Exegesis

Fortunately, exegesis for the preparation of a sermon does not involve the writing of one or two exegesis papers per week. Unfortunately, however, most theologically trained pastors, who learned to write exegesis papers for a course, were not likewise trained to apply those skills to the more common task of preparing a sermon. This chapter seeks to fill that void, by providing a handy format to follow for the exegesis of a NT passage, in order to preach confidently and competently from it.

Exegesis for a sermon is not different in kind from that required to write a paper, but it is different in its time requirements and its goal. This chapter, therefore, is a blended version of the full guide used for exegesis papers, outlined in Chapters I and II. (If for some reason some of those skills were never learned—or have become rusty—you may wish to block out some time during a week or two to go through those two chapters to "brush up" a bit.)

Although the process of exegesis itself cannot be redefined, the fashion in which it is done can be adjusted considerably. In the case of sermon preparation, exegesis cannot and, fortunately, need not be as exhaustive as that of the term paper. The fact that it cannot be exhaustive does not mean that it cannot be adequate. The goal of the shorter guide is to help the pastor extract from the passage the essentials pertaining to sound interpretation and exposition (explanation and application). The final product, the sermon, can and must be based on research that is reverent and sound in scholarship. The

145

sermon, as an act of obedience and worship, ought not to wrap shoddy scholarship in a cloak of fervency. Let your sermon be exciting, but let it be in every way faithful to God's revelation.

The chapter is divided into two parts: (1) a guide through the exegetical process itself; (2) some brief suggestions about moving from text to sermon, i.e., the actual preparation of the sermon. The guide is geared to the pastor who has ten hours or more per week for sermon preparation (approximately five for the exegesis and five or more for the sermon). Each section of the exegetical part of the guide contains a suggestion of the approximate time one might wish to devote to the issues raised in that section. Although the five hours were allotted somewhat arbitrarily, that would seem to be the minimum amount of time that a pastor ought to give to the research aspect of sermon preparation. Depending on the particular passage, the time available to you in a given week, and the nature of your familiarity with the text and the exegetical resources, you will find that you can make considerable adjustments in the time allotments. The actual time it takes beyond the exegesis for the writing of the sermon is such an individual matter that no times are given. The point here is that good, exegetically sound sermons can be produced in ten hours, and this guide hopes to help to that end.

As you become increasingly familiar with the steps and methods, you may arrive at a point where you can dispense with reference to the guide itself. That is the goal of this primer—that it should get you started, not that it should always be used.

A. THE EXEGETICAL TASK

Biblical preaching from the NT is, by definition, the task of bringing about an encounter between people of the present century and the Word of God—first spoken in the first century. The task of exegesis is to discover that Word and its meaning in the first-century church; the task of preaching is to know well *both* the exegesis of the text *and* the people to whom that Word is now to be spoken again, as a living Word for them.

The question is, where to begin. The obvious starting place, of course, is with the choice of text. But what guides that choice? Two things basically. Either (1) you are working your way through the biblical text and recognize the need to apply a given passage to your congregation, or (2) you recognize a certain need among the people and come to the Bible looking for a word that will address that need.

The outline that follows assumes the former approach, namely, that the biblical text itself determines the direction of the sermon.

But NOTE WELL: The great danger in preaching through a biblical book, or in letting the text determine the sermon, is that the sermon itself may become an exercise in exegesis. Such a "sermon" is exposition without aim, information without focus. That may be all right in the Sunday school class setting, where one simply goes through a passage, expounding and applying as one sees fit, but it is *not* preaching. Preaching must be *based* on solid exegesis, but it is not a display of exegesis. Rather, it is applied exegesis, and it must have aim if it is to function properly.

Throughout the exegetical task, therefore, you must constantly be working toward two ends: (1) to learn as much as you can about your text, its overall point, and how all the details go together to make that point (recognizing all along that not everything you learn will necessarily be included verbally in the sermon); (2) to think about the application of the text, which especially in this case includes the discriminating use of all that you have learned in the exegetical process. Let it be said now, and repeated throughout: You must overcome the urge to include everything in your sermon that you have learned in your exegesis; likewise you must overcome the urge to parade your exegesis and thus appear as the local guru.

The following steps will be regularly illustrated from two texts, one from the Epistles (1 Peter 2:18–25) and one from the Gospels (Mark 9:49–50). The former was chosen because of the hermeneutical issues involved (How do words to slaves in the first century speak to us today?); the latter because these are particularly difficult sayings of Jesus. It is hoped that one will not always neglect, or preach around, such texts as these.

1. Getting Started (*Allow approximately one hour and twenty minutes*)

It is imperative at the outset that you have a good preliminary sense of the context and content of your passage. To do this well you will need to do the following:

1.1. *Read the larger context.*

Do not be so anxious to get at the meaning of your text that you fail to take the time to have a good general sense as to where it fits in the biblical book you are preaching from. Always remember that your text is only one small part of a whole, and was never intended by the biblical author to be looked at or thought of independently from the rest of what he says.

You should therefore make it a regular practice to read your passage in its larger context. And then read it again—perhaps in a different translation the second time through. If you are dealing with one of the shorter Epistles, take the time to read the whole Epistle through, thinking carefully about the author's argument and how your passage fits in. If it is a longer Epistle, read and reread the section in which it is found (e.g., 1 Peter 1:1 to 3:12 or 22). If you are in the Gospels, select a logical larger section as your context (e.g., Mark 8:27–10:16—let the commentaries guide you here, if you must), and read and reread, so that you can easily retrace in your mind what goes before and what follows after your text.

NOTE: If you are setting out to preach your way through a biblical book, then you need to block out extra time at the beginning and work your way through Step 1 in Chapter I (I.1). Knowledge of the *whole* book must precede work on any of its parts.

1.2. Read the passage repeatedly.

Now do the same thing with your specific passage. Only this time you are reading and rereading for its basic *content*. Go over the passage out loud. Try to get a feel for it as a unit conveying God's Word to you and your congregation. Try to become sufficiently familiar with the passage so that you can keep its essentials in your head as you carry on through the next five steps. Perhaps you could read it through in a number of different translations—those that your congregation would know and use—and make a list of the significant differences (see step 3.3 in Chapter I). This would especially be helpful in situations where some in the congregation still revere the King James Version. Knowing beforehand where the KJV will differ from your translation can help you to anticipate some people's anxieties here.

Also be on the lookout for the possibility that you may need to adjust somewhat the limits of your passage, since the chapter and verse divisions as we have them are secondary to the composition of the original and are not always reliable. Check by starting a few verses before the beginning of the passage, and by going a few verses past the end. Adjust the limits if necessary (shrink or expand the passage to coincide with more natural boundaries if your sense of the passage so requires). It will be clear by this test, for example, that 1 Peter 2:18–25 is the unit one must work with. In the case of Mark 9:49–50 it will also become clear that this is something of a self-contained unit, held together by the word "salt." But the γάρ (for) in v. 49 also ties it directly to what has preceded, so that in this case one would do well to include vs. 42–48 in the exegetical work—even though you may limit the sermon to vs. 49–50. Once satisfied that the passage is properly delimited, and that you have a preliminary feel for its content and the way its words and thoughts flow, proceed to step 1.3, below.

1.3. Make your own translation.

Try this, even if your Greek is dormant or weak. For this task use one of the aids noted in IV.3. You can easily check yourself by referring whenever necessary to one or two of the better modern versions.

Making your own translation has several benefits. One is that it will help you to notice things about the passage that you would not notice in reading, even in the original. Much of what you begin to notice will anticipate steps 2.1 through 2.5, below. For example, you should begin to become alert to any textual questions that will affect the meaning of the text, to the special vocabulary of the passage, its grammatical features, and any historical-cultural issues, since all these matters are drawn naturally to your attention in the course of translating the words of the passage. Moreover, you are the expert on your congregation. You know its members' vocabulary and educational level(s), the extent of their biblical and theological awareness, etc. Indeed, you are the very person who is uniquely capable of producing a meaningful translation that you can draw upon in whole or in part during your sermon, to ensure that the congregation is really understanding the true force of the Word of God as the passage presents it.

[English Bible readers can substitute step 3.3 in Chapter I.]

1.4. Compile a list of alternatives.

In the process of making your own translation, you need to keep a list of translational alternatives that are textual, grammatical, or linguistic/stylistic in nature. The list need not be long; only significant items should be included. This list may then serve as a reference point for the items in step 2, below. For example, the list for Mark 9:42–50 should include the textual matters in vs. 42, 44, 46, and 49; the words σκανδαλίζω (offend, sin, stumble, undoing), γέεννα (hell), ἅλας (salt), ζωή = βασιλεία τοῦ θεοῦ (life = kingdom of God) in vs. 43, 45, 47; and the grammatical question related to γάρ (for) in v. 49. If you used the Good News Bible as one of your translations (step 1.3, above), you should also note on your list how that translation has interpreted the first and third of the salt sayings.

How many of these alternatives should be mentioned in the sermon will be a matter of personal judgment. In any case, err on the side of restraint, lest the sermon become cluttered. Some suggestions on textual items are given in 2.1, below. On other data it is a matter of the significance for understanding the passage. Sometimes you can simply choose your alternative as it appears in one of the translations and say, "As the RSV has it . . . " or "In my view the Good News Bible has the better of it here by translating . . . " If it is a more crucial issue, related to the meaning of the text, or especially related to the point you want to drive home, then it would be appropriate to give a brief summary of why you feel the evidence leads to your choice (or why you feel the evidence is not decisive).

1.5. *Analyze the structure.*

One further way of looking at the text in a preliminary fashion can also prove to be of immense value. It is important not only that you are aware of what details will need investigating, but also that you have a good sense of the structures of your passage and the flow of the argument. The best way to do this is to transcribe the Greek text into a sentence flow schematic as described in II.1.1. The great advantage of this exercise is that it helps you to visualize the structures of the paragraph, as well as forces you to make up your mind on several syntactical issues. In fact, almost always it will help you pick up items you missed even in translating.

Thus a sentence flow of 1 Peter 2:18–25 will help you to see not only that in vs. 18–20 the main point of the exhortation is to leave one's case with God when suffering unjustly, but also that the example of Christ given in vs. 21–25, which reinforces the exhortation, has two parts to it: (1) the fact that "Christ suffered *for you*" (v. 21) and at the same time (2) "left an *example* for you to follow" (v. 21). The four relative clauses that follow (which might be missed otherwise) then pick up these two themes: The first two (vs. 22–23) elaborate on his *example;* the second two (vs. 24a–b, 24c) expound on his suffering for them—and both of these in terms of Isaiah 53. To be sure, all of this could be seen simply by translating, but the sentence flow, especially when color-coded, makes it all readily visible.

1.6. *Start a sermon use list.*

In the same way that you compiled the list of alternatives mentioned in 1.4, above (and perhaps including that list), keep nearby a sheet of paper on which you record those observations from your exegetical work on the passage which you feel may be worth mentioning in your sermon. This list should include points discovered from all of steps 1–5 in this chapter; it will provide an easy reference as you construct the sermon itself.

What to include? Include the very things that you would feel cheated about if you did not know them. They need not be limited to genuine life-changing observations, but they should not be insignificant or arcane either. If something actually helps you appreciate and understand the text in a way that would not otherwise be obvious, then put it down on the mention list.

Maximize at first. Include anything that you feel deserves to be mentioned because your congregation might profit from knowing it. Later, when you actually write or outline your sermon, you may have to exclude some or most of the items on the mention list, because of the press of time. This will be especially so if your sermon is not from a more rigidly expository format. Moreover, in perspective you will undoubtedly see that certain items originally included for mention are not so crucial as you first thought. Or, conversely, you may find that you have so much of significance to draw to your congregation's attention that you will need to schedule two sermons on the passage to expound it properly.

Remember: Your mention list is not a sermon outline, any more than a stack of lumber is a house. The mention list is simply a tentative record of those exegetically derived observations that your congregation deserves to hear and may indeed benefit from knowing.

2. Matters of Content (*Allow approximately one hour*)

The steps in this section are related to the various kinds of details that make up the content of your passage, the *what* of the text. Basically these questions are fourfold for any NT passage: textual, grammatical, linguistic, historical-cultural.

2.1. *Check for significant textual issues.*

Refer to the textual apparatus in your NA[26]. Look specifically for textual variations that would affect the meaning of the text for your congregation in the English translation. These are the major textual variants. There is not much point in concerning yourself with the minor variants—those that would not make much difference in the English translations. Here it will be especially helpful to have read your passage through in the several English translations, as suggested in 1.2, above. Whenever the textual variation itself has been responsible for the differences, be sure this has been included in your list of alternatives (1.4, above). You will need to evaluate the major variations for yourself as to which is most likely the original and why (see II.2), especially so when there are differences in the translations the people might be using.

The question of how much, if any, of these things one will include in the sermon is a tricky one, for this is an area that can sometimes be upsetting to believers (it touches on the area of the *reliability* of Scripture for many). The rule is this: Seldom (almost never!) do textual criticism per se in the pulpit; that is, seldom, if ever, explain to the congregation how you arrived at a particular decision. You should include your reasoning only in the following situations: (1) When there are major textual decisions, and these are reflected in translations you know the people will be using (e.g., the RSV, KJV, and NIV on 1 Cor. 11:29). (2) When your own choice differs from the "pew Bible" of your congregation (this is especially so for those whose churches still generally use the KJV—but be careful of criticizing someone else's Bible!). (3) When a textual note will help to let the people see how the text was understood, or misunderstood, in the early church. For example, one can show how in Mark 9:49 the Western text was trying to alleviate what is otherwise a very difficult saying, but at the same time, by conforming the saying to Lev. 2:13, it has given considerable insight into the possible background for the original saying itself (the point picked up in the translation of the Good News Bible). This could be a part of your explanation of the text as you expound its meaning to the congregation.

On the other hand, the interchange between ὑμῶν (your) and ἡμῶν (our) in 1 Peter 2:21 may or may not be mentioned, depending upon whether you want to stress the point of Christ's having suffered for these Christian servants/slaves. In that case one could say something like: "In order to reinforce his point that these slaves should follow Christ's example, Peter also reminds them of the *effect* of Christ's suffering, namely, that it was *for them*. In some translations you will find v. 21 translated 'Christ suffered *for us*'—and while that is true and is picked up in v. 24, that misses Peter's point in v. 21. Here the older and more reliable evidence, which is picked up in most newer translations, is to be preferred as having the original text. . . . "

2.2. *Note any grammar that is unusual, ambiguous, or otherwise important.*

Your primary interest is to isolate grammatical features that might have some effect on the interpretation of the passage. Here in particular you will be learning more than you will have occasion to relate. For example, as you work with the ambiguous διὰ συνείδησιν θεοῦ (because he is conscious of God [NIV]; for the sake of conscience toward God [NASB]) in 1 Peter 2:19, you will need to make up your own mind as to the force of the genitive (cf. the commentaries of Davids and Michaels), but you will scarcely need to give any of the grammatical data to the congregation.

Sometimes, of course, an explanatory grammatical word can be especially helpful. The γάρ (for) in 1 Peter 2:25, for example, can be explained as being clearly explanatory, so that the "healing" of v. 24 must be a metaphor for salvation in this instance, not a reference to physical healing. Likewise the difference between an objective and a subjective genitive might be explained at times so that the force of *your* exegesis can be more clearly seen (see II.3.3.1). How one treats the γάρ in Mark 9:49 may vary. It would probably be appropriate to point out (perhaps in the sermon introduction) that by using this word Mark certainly *intended* to tie these sayings to what has preceded, but that it is not altogether clear *what* that connection is; later in the sermon, after you have given your interpretation of the text, you may wish to comment again on how these sayings can now be seen to relate to the sayings that have preceded them.

2.3. *Make a list of key terms.*

At this point you will want to go back to your list in 1.4, above, and reflect on it again, now in terms of key words that may need explanation at some point in the sermon. You may now wish to revise that list with these concerns in mind. For example, your preliminary list for 1 Peter 2:18–25 should probably include the following (from the NRSV): slaves, harsh, suffer, approval, called, example, wounds, healed, shepherd, guardian. Again, you will want to satisfy yourself as to the special nuances of all these words for the meaning of the passage, but you must not feel compelled to explain everything in the sermon. It would probably be of some importance, for example, to point out that even though οἰκέτης means household servant, such servants were almost invariably slaves; and it would surely be of some interest for the people to learn that the μώλωψ (wound) which Christ suffered for the salvation of these slaves is a word that referred to the black-and-blue welt that one received through whipping—which many of them had surely experienced (cf. v. 20).

2.4. *Do a mini word study for any crucial terms.*

Sometimes one or more of the words are of enough significance for your sermon that you will want to investigate them beyond the confines of the passage itself, in order better to understand what it means in your passage. "Salt" in Mark 9:49–50 is an obvious example; but because its meaning has ultimately to do with historical-cultural matters, we will hold it until 2.5, below. In 1 Peter 2:19–20, Peter's use of χάρις would be such a word. It is obviously being used in a sense considerably different from Paul's ordinary, and for most Christians the common, meaning. But does it mean "glory" (KJV), "credit" (NRSV), "commendable" (NIV), or "God will bless you" (GNB)?

For such a word study use the techniques described in II.4, but use your time wisely. By checking with Bauer and your Greek concordance you will be able quickly to discern its possible range(s) of meaning. You will want to note the usage in 1 Peter especially and how that usage differs considerably from Paul's. Here you will do your hearers a service by sharing with them a condensed form of some of the pertinent data. Paul's use of χάρις, after all, is not the only biblical one, and people need to be aware of that.

2.5. *Investigate important historical-cultural matters.*

Most people in a congregation are usually helped when you explain some of the historical-cultural matters that are truly significant to the meaning of the text. For the kinds of concerns that need to be investigated here, and some bibliographic suggestions, see II.5.

In the two example passages there are at least two such items in each that deserve some attention on your part. In Mark 9:42–50 it will probably be helpful for you to do a brief investigation of the term γέεννα (Gehenna = hell) and the forcefulness of the metaphor for these sayings. The term "salt" is of course the crucial one. Here your investigation of the use of salt in Jewish antiquity will probably be the key to your interpretation of all three sayings. Apparently three different uses are being metaphorically referred to in the three sayings: salt on sacrifices, salt for taste or preservative, and salt as a covenant bond.

In 1 Peter 2:18–25 you will want to spend a brief time reading about slaves—and their treatment—in the Greco-Roman world. Again, you will need a good sense of time as to how much you relate, but if the sermon is going to move adequately from the first to the present century, your congregation deserves to know something about the nature of first-century slavery—and how radical these words of exhortation would have been. Also it is of crucial importance to your exegesis to trace very carefully the use of Isaiah 53 in vs. 22–25. In this regard you may wish to consult one of the better studies on Christian midrashic techniques as they appear in the NT (see Bailey and Vander Broek, pp. 42–49 [IV.9.2]).

A caution here. Because this kind of information can be so fascinating, one can sometimes yield to the temptation to give it an inordinate amount of time in the sermon. Don't let such matters get in the way of the preaching so as to become all-absorbing. Let these, as with other matters, be useful servants for the proclamation of the Word, but don't let them rule.

3.   Contextual Questions (*Allow approximately one hour*)

To work out the matters of content is only half the exegetical task. Now you must give close attention to the questions of historical and literary context. Historical context has to do with the general historical milieu as well as with the specific occasion of the document. Literary context has to do with how your passage fits in specifically at its place in the argument or narrative.

Since the nature of the Gospels (see p. 45, above) requires one to look at these questions differently from the other genres, this section, as with Chapter I, will be divided into two parts, one for the Epistles (including Acts and Revelation) and one for the Gospels.

3 (E).   Epistles (Acts, Revelation)

For the exegesis of a passage from the Epistles you should familiarize yourself with the discussion at I.9–11 (E). For Acts see I.10–11 (A), and for Revelation see I.9–11 (R).

3.1 (E).   *Examine the historical context.*

This investigation has three parts to it. First, you need to learn something about the general situation of the recipients. If your passage is in one of the Pauline letters, spend a little time becoming

familiar with the city and its people. For this you should consult
either one of the better Bible dictionaries (see II.5.2.1) or the introduction to one of the better commentaries (see IV.13.3); if you have
time, interest, and available resources (a good library nearby), you
may pursue some of these matters further through the bibliography
provided in the dictionary article.

Beyond that you also need to familiarize yourself with the nature
and composition of the church(es) to which the Epistle was written.
Are they chiefly Jewish Christians, Gentiles, or some mixture? Is
there any inkling as to their socioeconomic status? Here again consult the introductions to the commentaries. But here also keep your
eyes open as you read the biblical text for yourself. For example, as
you read 1 Peter 1–3 through a couple of times (1.1, above), you
should have noted that the recipients are Gentile believers (1:18;
2:10; cf. 4:3) and that at least some of them are slaves and women
(2:18–3:7).

Finally, and most important, you need to reconstruct for yourself,
with the aid of your resources if necessary, the specific historical
situation that occasioned this section within the Epistle. This is one
of the absolutely crucial steps in the exegetical process, for your letter, after all, is a response to something. It is an immeasurable aid to
understanding to have worked out as carefully as possible what the
situation is that your Epistle addresses. You may get at this on your
own—if time allows—by listening carefully to the Epistle as you
read it through. But again, if necessary, consult the better commentaries; and since some of this work borders on speculation, you
would do well to compare two or three sources on this matter. Thus
for 1 Peter, although some of the details will differ from scholar to
scholar, it can be easily recognized that hostility from pagan sources
is the basic cause of the letter, and that our passage is a part of an
exhortation on how to respond as a Christian to a specific expression
of that hostility.

It is almost always appropriate to include this kind of material in
the sermon. This, above all else, will give your interpretation credi-
bility—when the text is seen as a response to a given situation.

3.2 (E). *Examine the literary context.*

For your specific text you have now come to the absolutely essential exegetical question. *What is the point* of this passage? How does
it fit into the overall scheme of the letter? And more important, how
does it fit right at this point in the author's argument or exhortation?
To do this well you need to take the time to write out on your ser-

mon use list (see 1.6, above) the two brief statements suggested in I.11 (E), namely: (1) the logic and content of your passage; (2) an explanation as to how this content contributes to the argument. This is the place where a lot of interpretation goes aground. Make a habit of forcing yourself always to do this—even if the commentaries do not always do so (this is also the place where many commentaries fail). Never be satisfied that you have done your exegesis until you have a measure of confidence that you can answer the question *why*, as well as the question *what*. There will be times, of course, when this is less clear (e.g., 2 Cor. 6:14 to 7:1), and you must be properly hesitant. But even in such cases, this question must always be wrestled with. For the sermon to have integrity as a proclamation of the *intent* of Scripture, it should focus on this question, and all its parts should serve that focus.

Thus a sermon on 1 Peter 2:18–25 should focus on the main point of the exhortation—leaving one's case with God in the face of hostility and cruelty—although how one goes about making that point, and bringing in Peter's supporting arguments, will be as varied as there are different preachers. You may, of course, wish to preach only from vs. 21–25, on Christ as Example and Savior, but even here you will want to set such a sermon in its literary context of vs. 18–25.

3 (G). Gospels

For the exegesis of a passage from the Gospels you should familiarize yourself with the discussion at I.9–11 (G) and II.6.

3.1 (G). *Identify the form.*

Do not spend a lot of time here. The important thing to note is that in the Gospels you have genres within the genre. Parables, for example, *function* in a certain way, as do proverbs, or hyperbole (Mark 9:43–48), or the narratives. For the literature on identifying the forms, see IV.9 (G). Again, this is not something one makes much of in the sermon itself, except perhaps to remind the people, for example, that a saying is proverbial and that proverbs function in a certain way (e.g., Mark 9:50a).

3.2 (G). *Use a synopsis.*

In order to get at the historical-literary context of a passage from the Gospels it is of greatest benefit for you to learn to study your passage from a Greek synopsis (from the Greek-English synopsis

[II.6.1] if your Greek is rusty). If you are not familiar with working with a synopsis, you will do yourself a lifetime favor if you will take the time to learn carefully the procedures outlined in II.6, especially II.6.3. What you are basically trying to discover here is how your Evangelist has put his Gospel together in the immediate area of your text; and very often this can be greatly helped by seeing how the other Evangelists treat the same material (whether dependent or independently).

Thus, for example, it should not be surprising that neither Matthew nor Luke totally follows Mark from 9:37 to 9:50 (there are some inherently difficult items here, as you will have sensed for yourself when reading it through). That neither Matthew nor Luke picks up the three salt sayings should surprise no one. On the other hand, you will receive some help in your interpretation of Mark 9:50a by recognizing that another version of that same (or a similar) saying existed in the double tradition. At least some of this kind of information, without long, dry treatises on the Synoptic problem and its solution, may well be a part of the sermon, both as helpful information and to reinforce your point about the inherent difficulty in understanding.

3.3 (G).   *Investigate possible life settings where appropriate.*

If it will be of some usefulness to the sermon, one may spend some time thinking about the possible original life setting of the passage in the ministry of Jesus (see I.11 [G] and IV.11 [G]). This will be especially true for many of the parables. In our present passage, however, very little is to be gained here, since it would be rather speculative at best and since the real contextual question here is the present literary one.

It is always appropriate to consider whether your passage contributes to the understanding of the Evangelist's life setting; or the other way about, whether that life setting (allowing for its hypothetical nature) adds to your understanding of the passage. If, as most believe, Mark's Gospel appeared in Rome during a time of suffering for the church, and discipleship for him entails following a suffering-servant Messiah (cf. Mark 8:27–38, etc.), then at least the first of these salt sayings fits nicely into this motif (following the second passion prediction) as a call to discipleship tried by fire.

3.4 (G).   *Describe the present arrangement or adaptation.*

Basically this step flows out of 3.2 (G), above. The procedure may be found in II.6.5–6. Here especially you will do far more learning for your own understanding of the text than you will find it necessary to include in the sermon. What you are looking for are those items that will give you insight into the author's emphases and his point in including the passage right here. Thus you are here going about answering the questions of literary context.

As it was relatively easy to determine the literary context of 1 Peter 2:18–25, so it is difficult to do so with Mark 9:49–50. It is always appropriate to be cautious at such points. Nonetheless, if you feel you can make good sense of the text in its context, then don't hesitate to say so, provided it is clear to all that you also have some reservations. Here especially you will want to seek the aid of the better commentaries.

4. Secondary Literature (*Allow approximately fifty minutes*)

You have now come to the conclusion of your basic work on the text itself. With the help of several exegetical aids you should feel that you have a good sense of understanding of the text, in both its particulars and its place in the biblical book. At this point you should take a little time to consult some secondary literature.

4.1. *Consult commentaries.*

Do not avoid commentaries; just be sure you do not read them through as the first order of business. If you do, you will always be preaching from someone else's work on the text, however good that may be, and never have confidence that the text is your own because you have mastered it. But now is the time to look at some commentaries. You should secure for your own library at least two or three of the very best available commentaries for each NT book (see IV.13.3). There are three reasons for reading the commentaries at this point: (1) To look at the options of scholars for some of the difficulties you had at various points in your exegesis. At times, of course, you will consult the commentaries when you meet the difficulty as you exegete the text. (2) To listen to at least three other interpretations of the text with which you can compare your own and make adjustments if another turns out to be more convincing. (3) To be alerted to issues or options that you overlooked in your exegesis that may prove to be crucial for your sermon. Thus, for example, reading through the commentaries of Kelly, Michaels, and Davids on 1 Peter 2:18–25 should not only increase your confidence in your own work but also aid your understanding of the text.

4.2. *Read other literature.*

This is the step that is conditioned by time, resources, and geography. There are times, such as while studying Mark 9:49–50, when you would like to read what others have written about those sayings. If such an opportunity arises, you need to consult the bibliographic aids in IV.13.1–2.

5. Biblical-Theological Context (*Allow approximately thirty minutes*)

Before you move on to the concerns of application, you need to think your way through how this passage relates to other Scripture and Christian theology.

5.1. *Analyze the passage's relation to the rest of Scripture.*

What is this passage similar or dissimilar to? Is it one of many similar types, or is it fairly unique? What gaps does it fill? Does anything hinge on it elsewhere? Do other Scriptures help make it comprehensible? How? Where does it fit in the overall structure of biblical revelation? What value does it have for the student of the Bible? In what ways is it important for your congregation?

Thus, for example, for 1 Peter 2:18–25 you will want to analyze briefly the similar passages in Paul (Eph. 6:5–9; Col. 3:22–4:1; 1 Tim. 6:1–2; Titus 2:9–10). It may be instructive to note that the Ephesian and Colossian passages assume Christian masters, while the others (including 1 Peter) assume Christian slaves and pagan masters.

5.2. *Analyze the passage's use in, and relation to, theology.*

To what theological doctrines does the passage add light? What are its theological concerns? Might the passage raise any questions or difficulties about some theological issue or stance that needs an explanation? How major or minor are the theological issues upon which the passage touches? Where does the passage seem to fit within the full system of truth contained in Christian theology? How is the passage to be harmonized with the greater theological whole? Are its theological concerns more or less explicit (or implicit)? How can you use the passage to help make your congregation more theologically consistent or, at least, more theologically alert?

6. Application (*Allow approximately forty minutes*)

You should have been thinking right along about how your passage and its various parts might apply to your own life and to that of the congregation. But now you should focus directly on application.

6.1. *List the life issues in the passage.*

Make a list of the possible life issues that are mentioned explicitly, referred to implicitly, or logically to be inferred from the passage. There may be only one or two of these, or there may be several. Be inclusive at first. Later you can eliminate those which, upon reflection, you judge to be less significant or irrelevant.

6.2. *Clarify the possible nature and area of application.*

Arrange your tentative list (mental or written) according to whether the passage or parts of it are in nature informative or directive, and then whether they deal with the area of faith or the area of action. While these distinctions are both artificial and arbitrary to some degree, they are often helpful. They may lead to more precise and specific applications of the Scripture's teaching for your congregation, and they will help you avoid the vague, general applications that are sometimes no applications at all.

6.3. *Identify the audience and categories of application.*

Are the life issues of the passage instructive primarily to individuals or primarily to corporate entities, or is there no differentiation? If to individuals, which? Christian or non-Christian? Clergy or lay? Parent or child? Strong or weak? Haughty or humble? If to corporate entities, which? Church? Nation? Clergy? Laity? A profession? A societal structure?

Are the life issues related to or confined to certain categories such as interpersonal relationships, piety, finances, spirituality, social behavior, family life?

B.   MOVING FROM EXEGESIS TO SERMON

What you have been doing to this point is *not* the sermon itself. You have been discovering the meaning of the text in terms of its original intent. In a certain sense that is the easier task compared to this second one—the actual preparation of the sermon. Here your best ally is a good head, with a lively imagination! In any case nothing can substitute for thinking. How do the exegetical insights and matters of application converge into a single sermon, with clear focus and specific aim? There can be no rules here, because a good sermon is as individual as you are. It must be *your* sermon, based on *your* exegesis, delivered to *your* congregation. What follows are simply some suggestions and cautions.

7.   Spend Some Time in Reflection on the Text and in Prayer.

Preaching is not simply an affair of the mind and study; it is also an affair of the heart and prayer. Once your mind is full of the text, its meaning, and some possible applications, take time to reflect on it prayerfully. How has the text addressed your own life? What needs of your own do you see being spoken to or met by this passage? Let there be time for you yourself to respond to the Word of God. It is very difficult to communicate as urgent to others what has not first spoken to oneself.

Then spend time reflecting on the text again, keeping in mind the various needs of the people in your congregation. How will you, by the help of the Holy Spirit in this sermon, be able to help, or encourage, or exhort them from this passage? Indeed the more time you spend *about* them in prayer over this passage, the more likely it is that you will prepare a sermon that will communicate *to* them.

Remember: Sermon preparation without personal encounter with the Word and without prayer will probably lack inspiration; and sermons preached by those who have not themselves sat in awful silence before the majesty of God and his Word will probably accomplish very little.

8.   Begin with a Sense of Purpose.

Drawing on your sermon use list and other notes you made to yourself as you were doing the exegesis, sit down at the beginning and hammer out three things (which will be subject to change, of course, as the sermon unfolds):

8.1.   *Main Points*

The *main point or points* of the biblical text that you need to proclaim. Your sermon needs *focus* or you will not know what you are trying to accomplish, and you will be difficult to follow. Try to decide what the congregation needs to know—or hear—from the passage, as opposed to what you needed to know to prepare the sermon. Your two best criteria here are the passage itself and your own response to it. What the passage treats as significant is probably what the sermon should treat as significant; what you feel is most helpful and important to you personally is probably what the congregation will find most helpful and important to them.

8.2. *Purpose*

The *purpose* of the present sermon. Here you want to decide *how* the above points will best be applicable. Is the sermon basically informational, dealing with the Christian faith? or is it exhortational, dealing with Christian behavior?

8.3. *Response*

The *response* that you hope the sermon will achieve. This is the other side of 8.2, above. Are you hoping to effect a change of thinking? or a change of behavior? or both? Are you trying to encourage? to motivate? to call for repentance? to bring people to an encounter with the living God? If the preacher's task is twofold, to comfort the afflicted and afflict the comfortable, which direction does this text take you? or will it be a bit of both?

NOTE: These last two items have to do with the *aim* of the sermon. A sermon that doesn't aim seldom hits a target. Deciding the *focus* and *aim* of the sermon will go a long way toward helping you decide how you will proceed with outline and content.

9. Decide on the Introduction and Conclusion.

The body, or content, of the sermon will in large measure be determined by how you plan to begin and end. The ending should be directed by the aim (8.2–3, above). Good sermons usually begin at one of three places: (1) with the biblical text itself—but be especially careful here lest you bore the people to death before you get to the application; (2) with the needs of the people in some way; or (3) in some imaginative way that catches their attention but will finally bring people and text together.

10. Construct an Outline.

By now an outline for the whole sermon should have emerged. Again there are no rules here; but caution is needed in several areas.

First, it is not necessary to follow the outline of the biblical text itself. That would be fine for a teaching setting, but a sermon is something else. Let the outline touch on the various points of the text, but let the logic of the presentation be your own, so as to build toward the conclusions you have set out in step 9, above.

Second, do not feel compelled to include in your sermon everything in the text. Be selective. Let everything you select serve the aim of the sermon.

Third, decide early on where the exegesis itself will fit into the sermon. It may serve as the introduction, of which the rest of the sermon will be application, picking up the several points of the exegesis; it may come later on, as you move from the present century back to the first, and then back to the present again. Or it may be referred to point by point as you go through the sermon. But remember that the sermon is *not* simply a rehash of the exegesis. To be biblical you must let your words be clothed in the authority of the Word as it is found in its first-century setting; but to be relevant you must make that Word come alive in your own setting.

11.   Construct the Sermon.

This again is a highly individual matter. Be judicious about the amount of data you include from your sermon use list. Remember that a well-told story (one that is relevant to the text!) will be remembered far longer than your finest prose. Be sure you do not go too long into the sermon without the break that a good, helpful illustration affords, both to illuminate your point and to relieve the minds of those who are trying to follow your logic. For help in this area, consult the better books on homiletics.

IV

AIDS AND RESOURCES FOR THE STEPS IN EXEGESIS

T HE PURPOSE OF THIS CHAPTER is to call attention to the various resources for NT exegesis. These are organized and selected to coordinate with the outline provided by Chapter I. In addition to the specific suggestions given here, the student should also secure one or more of the following bibliographic aids:

Joseph A. Fitzmyer, *An Introductory Bibliography for the Study of Scripture*; Subsidia Biblica, 3 (Rome: Biblical Institute Press, 1981). Abbreviated throughout as JAF.

Douglas J. Moo (ed.), *An Annotated Bibliography on the Bible and the Church* (Compiled for the Alumni Association of Trinity Evangelical Divinity School, Deerfield, Ill., 1986).

Daniel J. Harrington, *The New Testament: A Bibliography* (Wilmington, Del.: Michael Glazier, 1985).

Although each of these is now a bit dated (as will always be true of published bibliographies), especially in its selection of commentaries, the student or pastor would benefit greatly from having all three of these. The student or pastor needs to keep alert to the periodic publication of such bibliographies, which will supplement these three.

Although Moo is a bit limited in some areas of NT exegesis, it is included here because of its larger usefulness for those in pastoral ministry; it is also briefly annotated. Although unfortunately not annotated, Harrington's is an invaluable source for the whole broad range of New Testament studies, including materials especially pertinent to doing exegesis. Fitzmyer's *Introductory Bibliography* is currently the best of its kind for exegetical work; it covers the whole Bible, is more fully annotated, and includes titles in the major scholarly languages. Entries given below will focus chiefly on English titles.

A bibliography of a slightly different kind should also be noted, especially for those interested in research in New Testament and related fields:

> Robert J. Kepple, *Reference Works for Theological Research: An Annotated Selective Bibliographical Guide;* 2d ed. (Lanham, Md.: University Press of America, 1981).

You should also be aware of an especially useful guide to some of the steps outlined in this *Handbook,* which also takes the student by the hand and guides her or him through the tools with photographs and examples:

> Cyril J. Barber, *Introduction to Theological Research* (Chicago: Moody Press, 1982).

An increasingly large number of computer-aided research tools are now available. The more accessible and useful of these will also be listed in what follows. The most complete bibliography of such items for the biblical scholar and student is:

> John J. Hughes, *Bits, Bytes and Biblical Studies: A Resource Guide for the Use of Computers in Biblical and Classical Studies* (Grand Rapids: Zondervan Publishing House, 1987).

You should also note here the three books mentioned in the Preface, since they have useful sections that will supplement many of the exegetical steps listed in Chapter I. These three works will be referred to throughout this chapter by the authors' last names:

> Conzelmann-Lindemann = Hans Conzelmann and Andreas Lindemann, *Interpreting the New Testament: An Introduction to the Principles and Methods of N.T. Exegesis* (Peabody, Mass.: Hendrickson Publishers, 1988).
> Black-Dockery = David Alan Black and David S. Dockery (eds.), *New Testament Criticism and Interpretation* (Grand Rapids: Zondervan Publishing House, 1991).
> Kearley et al. = F. Furman Kearley, Edward P. Myers, and Timothy D. Hadley (eds.), *Biblical Interpretation, Principles and*

Practice: Studies in Honor of Jack Pearl Lewis (Grand Rapids: Baker Book House, 1986).

Step 1.   Historical Context in General

For a good overview of both the historical-sociological environment of the NT in general and the historical setting/theological perspective of each of the NT books in particular, see Parts 2 and 3 of Conzelmann-Lindemann (pp. 105–282). For further help in answering the questions at this step, one needs two kinds of books: First, one of the better Introductions, which deal with the variety of critical issues (see JAF 274–284). A good cross-confessional look at things may be obtained from the following three:

Donald A. Carson, Douglas J. Moo, Leon Morris, *An Introduction to the New Testament* (Grand Rapids: Zondervan Publishing House, 1992).

Werner G. Kümmel, *Introduction to the New Testament;* rev. Eng. ed., trans. by Howard Clark Kee (Nashville: Abingdon Press, 1975). [JAF 278]

Alfred Wikenhauser, *New Testament Introduction* (New York: Herder & Herder, 1958). [JAF 284]

Second, you need a good content-oriented survey. Here the options are several. The best of these combines the needed elements of a survey (interpretive discussions) with superb, and creatively fresh, discussions of the questions of introduction:

Luke T. Johnson, *The Writings of the New Testament, An Interpretation* (Philadelphia: Fortress Press, 1986).

The longtime standard, representing the consensus of NT scholarship, is:

Howard C. Kee, F. W. Young, K. Froelich, *Understanding the New Testament;* 4th ed. (Englewood Cliffs, N.J.: Prentice-Hall, 1983).

Still of great help, especially with the overall message of each NT book, and more conservative in its orientation, is:

Glenn W. Barker, William L. Lane, J. Ramsey Michaels, *The New Testament Speaks* (New York: Harper & Row, 1969).

STEP 2. Limits of the Passage

For a helpful discussion of this issue, which also spills over into Step 11, see:

Raymond C. Kelcy, "Identifying the Pericope and Its Context," in Kearley et al., pp. 73–81.

STEP 3. Paragraph Overview/Provisional Translation

The key to using the Greek text for exegesis is to keep reading it on a regular basis. There are three useful books, any one of which kept close at hand with your Greek NT will help you to read the Greek NT, as well as guide you in the making of a provisional translation:

Sakae Kubo, *A Reader's Greek-English Lexicon of the New Testament* (Berrien Springs, Mich.: Andrews University Press, 1971).
Fritz Rienecker and Cleon Rogers, *A Linguistic Key to the Greek New Testament* (Grand Rapids: Zondervan Publishing House, 1982). [JAF 211]
Max Zerwick and Mary Grosvenor, *A Grammatical Analysis of the Greek New Testament:* vol. I, *Gospels-Acts;* vol. II, *Epistles-Apocalypse* (Rome: Biblical Institute Press, 1974, 1979). [JAF 211]

Kubo's book gives the basic meaning of words as they appear in the NT text. It is based on word frequency: Words occurring over 50 times in the NT are assumed to be known (but are listed in Appendix I). Words that occur from 6 to 50 times are listed at the beginning of each biblical book and form that author's "special vocabulary." Then are listed by chapter and verse all words that occur five times or less in any NT book. One of the helpful features of Kubo is that word frequencies (how many occurrences in a book/how many in the NT) are given for each word.

Either Rienecker-Rogers or Zerwick-Grosvenor should prove to be more useful, however, for the work of rapid reading and provisional translation. Rienecker-Rogers tends to give more lexical help, while Zerwick-Grosvenor, which is keyed to Zerwick's Greek grammar (see II.3.2.3), includes more grammatical analysis.

For an overview of the science of translation and the reason for the choice of the translations suggested in I.3.3, see Chapter 2 ("The Basic Tool—A Good Translation") in:

Gordon D. Fee and Douglas Stuart, *How to Read the Bible for All Its Worth*, 2d ed. (Grand Rapids: Zondervan Publishing House, 1993).

Step 4.   Sentence Flow or Diagram

See II.1.1 and II.1.2 for the few bibliographic resources suggested for use in making the sentence flow or diagram. An introductory discussion to the matters related to sentence analysis and diagraming can also be found in:

F. Furman Kearley, "Diagramming and Sentence Analysis," in Kearley et al., pp. 82–90.

[ENGLISH BIBLE READERS, those whose difficulties here are the result of a poor knowedge of English grammar, can find significant help in consulting the brief but thorough overview in:

H. P. V. Nunn, *A Short Syntax of New Testament Greek* (Cambridge: Cambridge University Press, 1965), pp. 1–24.

Those who wish to do this work from a very literal English "translation" should use:

J. D. Douglas (ed.), *The New Greek-English Interlinear New Testament* (Wheaton, Ill.: Tyndale House Publishers, 1990).]

Step 5.   Textual Criticism

In addition to the full discussion in II.2, see JAF, chapters IV–VI; Conzelmann-Lindemann, pp. 17–26 (for another useful "hands-on" approach); chapter 4 in Black-Dockery (by Michael W. Holmes, pp. 101–134); and chapter 16 in Kearley et al. (by Frank Pack, pp. 214–225). Note also the following:

Kurt Aland and Barbara Aland, *Text of the New Testament: An Introduction to the Critical Editions and to the Theory and Practice of Modern Textual Criticism*; 2d ed.; trans. by E. F. Rhodes (Grand Rapids: Wm. B. Eerdmans Publishing Co., 1989).

Gordon D. Fee, "The Textual Criticism of the New Testament," in *The Expositor's Bible Commentary*, ed. by Frank E. Gaebelein (Grand Rapids: Zondervan Publishing House, 1979), vol. 1, pp. 419–433.

J. Harold Greenlee, *Introduction to New Testament Textual Criticism* (Grand Rapids: Wm. B. Eerdmans Publishing Co., 1964), pp. 107–113. [JAF 89]

Bruce M. Metzger, *The Text of the New Testament: Its Transmission, Corruption, and Restoration;* 2d ed. (New York: Oxford University Press, 1968). [JAF 94]

————, *A Textual Commentary on the Greek New Testament* (New York: United Bible Societies, 1971), pp. xiii–xxxi.

STEP 6.   Grammar

In addition to the full discussion of the various tools in II.3, see JAF, pp. 59–62. Chapter 18 in Kearley et al. (by C. D. Osburn, pp. 234–243) offers some helpful illustrations of grammar and interpretation at work.

For those who use a computer, there is an especially useful grammatical concordance on software, by which one can search for almost any imaginable combination of grammatical possibilities in the NT. This is especially helpful in trying to determine a given author's usage elsewhere, so that all of the further examples of the grammatical matter you are working on can be seen at the same time. See:

Paul A. Miller (director), *Gramcord* (1984; The Gramcord Institute, 2218 NE Brookview Dr., Vancouver, WA 98686).

For the following items see the discussion in II.3:

John Beekman and John Callow, *Translating the Word of God* (Grand Rapids: Zondervan Publishing House, 1974), pp. 249–266.

Friedrich Blass and Albert Debrunner, *A Greek Grammar of the New Testament and Other Early Christian Literature;* trans. and rev. by Robert W. Funk (Chicago: University of Chicago Press, 1961). [JAF 203]

James A. Brooks and Carlton L. Winbery, *Syntax of New Testament Greek* (Lanham, Md.: University Press of America, 1979).

Ernest D. Burton, *Syntax of the Moods and Tenses in New Testament Greek;* 3d ed. (Edinburgh: T. & T. Clark, 1898; repr. Grand Rapids: Kregel Publications, 1976).

William D. Chamberlain, *An Exegetical Grammar of the Greek New Testament* (New York: Macmillan Co., 1961).

H. E. Dana and J. R. Mantey, *A Manual Grammar of the New Testament* (New York: Macmillan Co., 1927).

Robert W. Funk, *A Beginning-Intermediate Grammar of Hellenistic Greek;* 2d ed.; 3 vols. (Missoula, Mont.: Scholars Press, 1973).

Murray J. Harris, "Appendix: Prepositions and Theology in the Greek New Testament," in *The New International Dictionary of New Testament Theology,* ed. by Colin Brown (Grand Rapids: Zondervan Publishing House, 1978), vol. 3, pp. 1171–1215.

C. F. D. Moule, *An Idiom Book of New Testament Greek;* 2d ed. (Cambridge: Cambridge University Press, 1963). [JAF 207]

James H. Moulton and W. F. Howard, *A Grammar of New Testament Greek* (Edinburgh: T. & T. Clark): vol. I, *Prolegomena,* by Moulton, 3d ed., 1908; vol. II, *Accidence and Word-Formation,* by Moulton and Howard, 1929; vol. III, *Syntax,* by Nigel Turner, 1963; vol. IV, *Style,* by Turner, 1976. [JAF 208]

A. T. Robertson, *A Grammar of the Greek New Testament in the Light of Historical Research;* 4th ed. (Nashville: Broadman Press, 1934). [JAF 209]

—— and W. H. Davis, *A New Short Grammar of the Greek Testament;* 10th ed. (New York: Harper & Brothers, 1933; repr. Grand Rapids: Baker Book House, 1977).

Max Zerwick, *Biblical Greek Illustrated by Examples* (Rome: Biblical Institute Press, 1963). [JAF 212]

Step 7. Lexical Aids

For this material see JAF, pp. 51–54. For further help in using these materials see Cyril Barber, *Introduction to Theological Research,* pp. 81–101; and chapter 17 in Kearley et al. (by Leon Crouch, pp. 226–233). The materials listed below are discussed in II.4:

Kurt Aland (ed.), *Vollständige Konkordanz zum griechischen Neuen Testament;* 2 vols. (Berlin: Walter de Gruyter, 1975, 1983). [JAF 226]

John R. Alsop, *An Index to the Revised Bauer-Arndt-Gingrich Greek Lexicon;* 2d ed. (Grand Rapids: Zondervan Publishing House, 1981).

H. Bachmann and H. Slaby (eds.), *Computer-Konkordanz zum Novum Testamentum Graece von Nestle-Aland, 26. Auflage, und zum Greek New Testament,* 3rd ed. (Berlin: Walter de Gruyter, 1980).

Walter Bauer, *A Greek-English Lexicon of the New Testament and Other Early Christian Literature;* 2d ed.; ed. by W. F. Arndt, F. W. Gingrich, F. W. Danker (Chicago: University of Chicago Press, 1979). [JAF 173]

Colin Brown (ed.), *The New International Dictionary of New Testament Theology;* 3 vols. (Grand Rapids: Zondervan Publishing House, 1975–1978). [JAF 251]

Albert-Marie Denis, *Concordance Grecque des Pseudépigraphes d'Ancien Testament* (Louvain: Université Catholique de Louvain, 1987).

J. D. Douglas (ed.), *The New Greek-English Interlinear New Testament* (Wheaton, Ill.: Tyndale House Publishers, 1990).

Barbara and Timothy Friberg, *Analytical Concordance of the Greek New Testament—Lexical Focus* (Grand Rapids: Baker Book House, 1981).

G. H. R. Horsely (ed.), *New Documents Illustrating Early Christianity: A Review of the Greek Inscriptions and Papyri;* 5 vols. (North Ryde, Australia: Ancient History Documentary Research Centre, Macquarie University, 1981–1989).

Gerhard Kittel and Gerhard Friedrich (eds.), *Theological Dictionary of the New Testament;* 10 vols. including Index Volume (Grand Rapids: Wm. B. Eerdmans Publishing Co., 1964–1976). [JAF 252]

G. W. H. Lampe (ed.), *A Patristic Greek Lexicon* (Oxford: Clarendon Press, 1961–1968). [JAF 178]

Henry G. Liddell and Robert Scott, *A Greek-English Lexicon;* 9th ed.; rev. by H. S. Jones and R. McKenzie (Oxford: Clarendon Press, 1940). [JAF 179]

G. Mayer, *Index Philoneus* (Berlin: Walter de Gruyter, 1974).

James H. Moulton and G. Milligan, *The Vocabulary of the Greek Testament: Illustrated from the Papyri and Other Non-Literary Sources* (London: Hodder & Stoughton, 1914–1930; repr. Grand Rapids: Wm. B. Eerdmans Publishing Co., 1974; repr. New York: Gordon Press Publications, 1977). [JAF 180]

William F. Moulton and A. S. Geden, *A Concordance to the Greek Testament According to the Texts of Westcott and Hort, Tischendorf and the English Revisers;* 5th rev. ed. by H. K. Moulton (Edinburgh: T. & T. Clark, 1978). [JAF 228]

K. H. Rengstorf (ed.), *A Complete Concordance to Flavius Josephus;* 4 vols. (Leiden: E. J. Brill, 1973–). [JAF 455]

James Strong, *Exhaustive Concordance of the Bible* (Nashville: Abingdon Press, 1980).

Two computer-aided research tools now provide one with absolutely exhaustive "concordances" to all uses of Greek words, both literary and nonliterary. See:

Thesaurus Linguae Graecae [TLG] (computer data bank), Prof. Theodore F. Brunner, Director; University of California–Irvine; Irvine, CA 92717. Tel. (714) 856–6404.

Duke Data Bank of Documentary Papyri [DDBDP], Prof. William H. Willis, Director; Duke University; Box 4762 Duke Station; Durham, NC 27706. Tel. (919) 684–5076.

Step 8. Historical-Cultural Background

For these materials see JAF, pp. 113–132; see also the helpful discussions in Conzelmann-Lindemann, pp. 105–157 (esp. pp. 106–113 for helpful remarks on "sources") and Black-Dockery, pp. 349–376 (by David E. Garland). The materials listed below are discussed in II.5:

H. Almquist, *Plutarch und das Neue Testament. Ein Beitrag zum Corpus Hellenisticum Novi Testamenti;* Acta Seminarii Neotestamentici Upsaliensis, 15 (Uppsala: Appelbergs Boktryckeri, 1946).

Hans Dieter Betz, *Plutarch's Theological Writings and Early Christian Literature;* Studia ad Corpus Hellenisticum Novi Testamenti, 3 (Leiden: E. J. Brill, 1975).

———, *Plutarch's Ethical Writings and Early Christian Literature;* Studia ad Corpus Hellenisticum Novi Testamenti, 4 (Leiden: E. J. Brill, 1978).

———, *Lukian von Samosata und das Neue Testament. Religionsgeschichtliche und paränetische Parallelen;* Texte und Untersuchungen, 76 (Berlin: Akademie-Verlag, 1961).

——— and E. W. Smith, Jr., "Contributions to the Corpus Hellenisticum Novi Testamenti; I: Plutarch, De E apud Delphos," *Novum Testamentum* 13 (1971): 217–235.

J. Bonsirven, *Textes Rabbiniques des deux premiers siècles chrétiens pour servir à l'intelligence du Nouveau Testament* (Rome: Biblical Institute Press, 1955). [JAF 489]

H. Braun, *Qumran und das Neue Testament;* 2 vols. (Tübingen: J. C. B. Mohr [Paul Siebeck], 1966), vol. 2.

Geoffrey W. Bromiley et al. (eds.), *The International Standard Bible Encyclopedia;* rev. ed.; 4 vols. (Grand Rapids: Wm. B. Eerdmans Publishing Co., 1979-1988).

George A. Buttrick et al. (eds.), *The Interpreter's Dictionary of the Bible;* 4 vols. (Nashville: Abingdon Press, 1962). [JAF 240]

J. H. Charlesworth (ed.), *The Old Testament Pseudepigrapha;* 2 vols. (Garden City, N.Y.: Doubleday & Co., 1983–1985). [JAF 446]

Keith Crim et al. (eds.), *The Interpreter's Dictionary of the Bible, Supplementary Volume* (Nashville: Abingdon Press, 1976). [JAF 240]

J. Duncan M. Derrett, *Jesus's Audience: The Social and Psychological Environment in Which He Worked* (New York: Seabury Press, 1973).

André Dupont-Sommer, *The Essene Writings from Qumran* (Oxford: Basil Blackwell, 1961; repr. Gloucester, Mass.: Peter Smith, 1973). [JAF 447]

Everett Ferguson, *Backgrounds of Early Christianity* (Grand Rapids: Wm. B. Eerdmans Publishing Co., 1987).

David Noel Freedman (ed.), *The Anchor Bible Dictionary;* 6 vols. (New York: Doubleday & Co., 1992).

Martin Hengel, *Judaism and Hellenism: Studies in Their Encounter in Palestine During the Early Hellenistic Period;* 2 vols. (Philadelphia: Fortress Press, 1974). [JAF 400]

Joachim Jeremias, *Jerusalem in the Time of Jesus: An Investigation Into Economic and Social Conditions During the New Testament Period* (Philadelphia: Fortress Press, 1967). [JAF 534]

Eduard Lohse, *The New Testament Environment* (Nashville: Abingdon Press, 1976).

Victor H. Matthews, *Manners and Customs in the Bible: An Illustrated Guide to Daily Life in Bible Times* (Peabody, Mass.: Hendrickson Publishers, 1988).

Madeleine S. Miller and J. Lane Miller, *Harper's Encyclopedia of Bible Life;* 3d rev. ed. by Boyce M. Bennett and David H. Scott (New York: Harper & Row, 1978).

R. C. Musaph-Andriesse, *From Torah to Kabbalah: A Basic Introduction to the Writings of Judaism* (New York: Oxford University Press, 1982).

G. Mussies, *Dio Chrysostom and the New Testament: Parallels Collected* (Leiden: E. J. Brill, 1971).

Jacob Neusner, *The Rabbinic Traditions About the Pharisees Before 70 A.D.;* 3 vols. (Leiden: E. J. Brill, 1971). [JAF 493]

George W. E. Nickelsburg, *Jewish Literature Between the Bible and the Mishnah: An Historical and Literary Introduction* (Philadelphia: Fortress Press, 1981).

G. Petzke, *Die Traditionen über Apollonius von Tyana und das Neue Testament;* Studia ad Corpus Hellenisticum Novi Testamenti, 1 (Leiden: E. J. Brill, 1970).

Emil Schürer, *The History of the Jewish People in the Age of Jesus Christ (175 B.C.–A.D. 135): A New English Version Revised and Edited;* ed. by Géza Vermès et al.; 3 vols. (Edinburgh: T. & T. Clark, 1973, 1979). [JAF 410]

J. N. Sevenster, *Paul and Seneca;* Supplements to *Novum Testamentum,* 4 (Leiden: E. J. Brill, 1961).

Hermann L. Strack and Paul Billerbeck, *Kommentar zum Neuen Testament aus Talmud und Midrasch;* 6 vols. (Munich: Beck, 1922–1961). [JAF 496]

Hildegard Temporini and Wolfgang Haase (eds.), *Aufstieg und Niedergang der römischen Welt. Geschichte und Kultur Roms im Spiegel der neueren Forschung* (Berlin: Walter de Gruyter, 1972–).

J. A. Thompson, *Handbook of Life in Bible Times* (Downers Grove, Ill.: Inter-Varsity Press, 1986).

P. W. van der Horst, "Musonius Rufus and the New Testament: A Contribution to the Corpus Hellenisticum," *Novum Testamentum* 16 (1974): 306–315.

Step 9 (E). Epistolary Forms

9.1. For the seminal discussion of these matters, see:

Adolf Deissmann, *Light from the Ancient East: The New Testament Illustrated by Recently Discovered Texts of the Graeco-Roman World;* [1st ed., 1910] 4th ed. (New York: Harper & Brothers, 1922; repr. Grand Rapids: Baker Book House, 1965), esp. pp. 227–251. [JAF 548]

The best overviews of the NT Epistles in the context of ancient letter writing are in the Westminster Press series, the Library of Early Christianity (LEC), ed. by Wayne A. Meeks:

David E. Aune, *The New Testament in Its Literary Environment;* Library of Early Christianity, vol. 8 (Philadelphia: Westminster Press, 1987), pp. 158–225.

Stanley K. Stowers, *Letter Writing in Greco-Roman Antiquity;*
Library of Early Christianity, vol. 5 (Philadelphia: Westminster Press, 1986).

For another brief but helpful study, see:

William G. Doty, *Letters in Primitive Christianity;* Guides to
Biblical Scholarship (Philadelphia: Fortress Press, 1973).

For a very helpful discussion of the use of secretaries to write
letters in antiquity, see:

Gordon J. Bahr, "Paul and Letter Writing in the First Century,"
Catholic Biblical Quarterly 28 (1966): 465–477.

9.2.   The essential book for the various kinds of "forms" found
in the Pauline letter tradition is:

James L. Bailey and Lyle D. Vander Broek, *Literary Forms in the
New Testament: A Handbook* (Louisville, Ky.: Westminster/
John Knox Press, 1992), pp. 21–87.

After an opening chapter which looks at the various "parts" of the
Pauline letter (I.9.2 [E]), the chapters take up in turn Forms of Argu-
mentation (Rhetoric), the Diatribe, Midrash, Chiasm, Apocalyptic
Language and Forms, Paraenesis/Topoi, Vice and Virtue Lists, The
Household Code, Liturgical Fragments: Blessings and Doxologies,
Poetry and Hymn, and Creeds.

For a *collection* of these kinds of materials from the Greco-Roman
world, see:

Abraham J. Malherbe, *Moral Exhortation, A Greco-Roman
Sourcebook;* Library of Early Christianity, vol. 4 (Philadelphia: Westminster Press, 1986).

For introductory overviews of matters of rhetoric and style, see
Black-Dockery, pp. 227–254 (by A. Besançon Spencer) and pp. 518–
523 (by Craig L. Blomberg). The two more significant studies of the
possible use by the NT letter writers of rhetorical argumentation are
(although both authors probably overplay their hands on these matters):

George A. Kennedy, *New Testament Interpretation Through Rhetorical Criticism* (Chapel Hill, N.C.: University of North Car-
olina Press, 1984).

Burton L. Mack, *Rhetoric and the New Testament;* Guides to Biblical Scholarship (Minneapolis: Fortress Press, 1990).

STEP 10 (E).   Historical Context in Particular

Since this step has to do with the occasion of the letter, no special bibliography is available, although help may be obtained from the introductions in the commentaries, and sometimes from specialized studies. These will be discovered in the process of accumulating your bibliography for the specific Epistle being studied.

STEP 11 (E).   Literary Context

The biblical text itself provides the literary context. Hence no bibliography is necessary.

STEP 9 (G).   Gospel Forms

For a helpful introduction to the various matters that go into the exegesis of the Gospels, see:

Scot McKnight, *Interpreting the Synoptic Gospels;* Guides to New Testament Exegesis (Grand Rapids: Baker Book House, 1988).

The analysis of the "forms" of the materials found in the Gospels was a part of the investigation known as form criticism. Historically, this discipline arose as an attempt to study the Gospel materials as they were in the oral period before the first of our written Gospels. The formal analysis was part of an attempt to discover the original life setting of the saying or pericope and to judge its authenticity. The classification and analysis of the forms, however, exists quite apart from the latter concerns.

For a brief overview of form criticism, see Conzelmann-Lindemann, pp. 59–82; Black-Dockery, pp. 175–196 (by D. L. Bock). For helpful introductions and assessments of form criticism itself, see either:

William Barclay, *Introduction to the First Three Gospels* (rev. ed. of *The First Three Gospels*) (Philadelphia: Westminster Press, 1975), pp. 24–81.

or:

Keith F. Nickle, *The Synoptic Gospels: An Introduction* (Atlanta: John Knox Press, 1980), pp. 29–51.

Nickle's survey has an especially helpful presentation of the forms. On the matter of forms themselves, see also:

James L. Bailey and Lyle D. Vander Broek, *Literary Forms in the New Testament: A Handbook* (Louisville, Ky.: Westminster/ John Knox Press, 1992), pp. 91–166.

A more complete introduction to form criticism as such, but not as helpful as Nickle or Barclay on the forms, may be found in:

Edgar V. McKnight, *What Is Form Criticism?;* Guides to Biblical Scholarship (Philadelphia: Fortress Press, 1969).

More complete analysis of the forms, as well as a complete presentation of the Gospel materials, may be found in the classic work on form criticism:

Rudolf Bultmann, *The History of the Synoptic Tradition* (Oxford: Basil Blackwell, 1963).

Bultmann was excessively skeptical about authenticity, but his analysis of the forms and development of the tradition may be very useful. Barclay's introduction noted above is a careful, critical assessment of this book. A more balanced approach to the subject is:

Vincent Taylor, *The Formation of the Gospel Tradition;* 2d ed. (London: Macmillan & Co., 1935).

A brief analysis of the form of Jesus' teaching, which approaches the question of form in a slightly different but refreshing way, is:

Robert H. Stein, *The Method and Message of Jesus' Teachings* (Philadelphia: Westminster Press, 1978), pp. 7–33.

Step 10 (G).   Pericope Analysis

For an overview of the concerns that go into this analysis see Conzelmann-Lindemann, pp. 82–87. The following items are discussed in II.6.

Kurt Aland (ed.), *Synopsis Quattuor Evangeliorum;* 9th ed. (Stuttgart: Deutsche Bibelstiftung, 1976). [JAF 125]

———— (ed.), *Synopsis of the Four Gospels: Greek-English Edition of the Synopsis Quattuor Evangeliorum;* 3d ed. (New York: United Bible Societies, 1979). [JAF 124]

Albert Huck, *Synopsis of the First Three Gospels;* 13th ed., rev. by Heinrich Greeven (Tübingen: J. C. B. Mohr [Paul Siebeck], 1981).

Reuben J. Swanson, *The Horizontal Line Synopsis of the Gospels, Greek Edition* (Pasadena, Calif.: William Carey Library, 1984).

Step 11 (G).   The Original Life Setting

For an introduction to the problem here, see the bibliography given at Step 9 (G), above. A classic example of this kind of study at work is:

Joachim Jeremias, *The Parables of Jesus;* rev. ed. (New York: Charles Scribner's Sons, 1963).

For an approach to the material by way of audience, see:

J. Arthur Baird, *Audience Criticism and the Historical Jesus* (Philadelphia: Westminster Press, 1969), esp. pp. 32–53.

Step 10 (A).   Historical Questions

For an overview of the question of Luke-Acts and ancient historiography, see:

David E. Aune, *The New Testament in Its Literary Environment;* Library of Early Christianity, vol. 8 (Philadelphia: Westminster Press, 1987), pp. 77–157.

For the basic historical questions asked at this step (who, what, where, when), one should consult one of the better Bible dictionaries. See II.5.2.1 (cf. JAF, chapter XI).

For the broader and more complex question of history in Acts, see:

Martin Hengel, *Acts and the History of Earliest Christianity* (Philadelphia: Fortress Press, 1980).

I. Howard Marshall, *Luke: Historian and Theologian* (Grand Rapids: Zondervan Publishing House, 1971).

Step 11 (A).   Literary Context

No bibliography necessary. However, for two commentaries that approach exegesis with these questions in mind, see one that does not take the history seriously:

Ernst Haenchen, *The Acts of the Apostles, A Commentary* (Philadelphia: Westminster Press, 1971).

and one that does:

I. Howard Marshall, *The Acts of the Apostles;* Tyndale New Testament Commentaries (Grand Rapids: Wm. B. Eerdmans Publishing Co., 1980).

Step 9 (R).   Apocalyptic Form

On the question of the form of the Apocalypse, with further helpful bibliography, see especially:

David E. Aune, *The New Testament in Its Literary Environment;* Library of Early Christianity, vol. 8 (Philadelphia: Westminster Press, 1987), pp. 226–252.

Step 12.   Biblical Theology

Although NT theology is primarily a descriptive task, the presuppositions and prior theological commitments of the author often affect the way he or she sees things. Therefore it seems useful here to present the major NT theologies under confessional categories, with the caveat that one not read only from one's own point of view. There is much that can be learned from all of the theologies listed here (cf. Harrington, *The New Testament: A Bibliography,* pp. 143–191; JAF 345–354).

From the perspective of a more radical, in this case existential, point of view, see:

Rudolf Bultmann, *Theology of the New Testament;* 2 vols. (New York: Charles Scribner's Sons, 1951–1955). [JAF 345]

Hans Conzelmann, *An Outline of the Theology of the New Testament* (New York: Harper & Row, 1969). [JAF 346]

Bultmann's work is something of a classic and is especially full of insights on Paul. From a more moderate theological stance, see:

Leonhard Goppelt, *Theology of the New Testament:* vol. I, *The Ministry of Jesus in Its Theological Significance;* vol. II, *The Variety and Unity of the Apostolic Witness to Christ* (Grand Rapids: Wm. B. Eerdmans Publishing Co., 1981–). [JAF 347]

Werner G. Kümmel, *The Theology of the New Testament* (Nashville: Abingdon Press, 1973). [JAF 349]

Ethelbert Stauffer, *New Testament Theology* (London: SCM Press, 1955). [JAF 354]

From a conservative point of view, see:

Donald Guthrie, *New Testament Theology* (Downers Grove, Ill.: Inter-Varsity Press, 1981).

George E. Ladd, *A Theology of the New Testament* (Grand Rapids: Wm. B. Eerdmans Publishing Co., 1974).

The best from the Roman Catholic tradition is:

Karl H. Schelkle, *Theology of the New Testament;* 4 vols. (Collegeville, Minn.: Liturgical Press, 1971–1978). [JAF 352]

Since Paul and John receive so much attention in their own right, you should be aware of the better theologies here. For Paul see:

J. Christiaan Beker, *Paul the Apostle* (Philadelphia: Fortress Press, 1980).

Herman Ridderbos, *Paul: An Outline of His Theology* (Grand Rapids: Wm. B. Eerdmans Publishing Co., 1975).

The classic study for John is:

C. H. Dodd, *The Interpretation of the Fourth Gospel* (Cambridge: Cambridge University Press, 1953).

For a brief compendium of Johannine thought, see:

G. R. Beasley-Murray, *Gospel of Life: Theology in the Fourth Gospel* (Peabody, Mass.: Hendrickson Publishers, 1991).

For an overview of scholarly research on the theology of John, see:

Robert Kysar, *The Fourth Evangelist and His Gospel: An Examination of Contemporary Scholarship* (Minneapolis: Augsburg Publishing House, 1975), esp. Part Three, pp. 174–263.

STEP 13. **Secondary Literature**

Large numbers of valuable articles and books are published every year in the NT field. It is especially important that you know where such articles and books can be found and how to go about locating what you are looking for in this vast array of material. Since this has already been done well by Fitzmyer, pp. 1–21, here I will simply call your attention to the more significant items with very little annotation.

13.1. *Bibliographic Aids*

The first task, and the one that lightens the load considerably when one knows precisely where to look, is the accumulation of a bibliography. In the NT field we are richly served at this point. See especially chapter I(C) of JAF. The more significant published bibliographies that deal directly with NT exegesis are those on Christ and the Gospels by Metzger (JAF 16), on Paul by Metzger (JAF 17), on Acts by the Mattills (JAF 14), on John by Malatesta, and on "Festschriften" by Metzger (JAF 15). For current bibliography there are two absolutely indispensable tools:

Elenchus bibliographicus biblicus [JAF 6]
New Testament Abstracts [JAF 18]

You simply cannot expect to do serious and up-to-date work on anything in the NT without access to these two invaluable tools.

13.2. *Periodicals*

For the vast array of periodical literature that has scholarly articles on NT subjects, see chapter II in JAF. The more significant ones for NT study are:

Biblica [JAF 33]
Catholic Biblical Quarterly [JAF 37]
Expository Times [Not listed in JAF, but frequently it has some
   good quality articles]
Interpretation [JAF 40]
Journal of Biblical Literature [JAF 41]
Journal for the Study of the New Testament [JAF 42]
New Testament Studies [JAF 44]
Novum Testamentum [JAF 45]
Revue Biblique [JAF 47]
Zeitschrift für die neutestamentliche Wissenschaft [JAF 55]

13.3. *Commentaries*

For a list of commentary series, see JAF, pp. 87–90. For a helpful listing of the best NT commentaries for each of the NT books (through 1985), see Harrington, *The New Testament: A Bibliography*. It must be remembered of course that good new commentaries appear with regularity. The list given below is my own judgment as to the three (sometimes four) best commentaries (in English) for each NT book as of the writing of the second edition of this *Handbook*. Beyond that date see the notices of new books in *New Testament Abstracts*.

Series abbreviations:

AB	Anchor Bible (Doubleday)
EBC	Expositor's Bible Commentary (Zondervan)
Herm	Hermeneia (Fortress)
HNTC	Harper's New Testament Commentaries (Harper & Row)
ICC	International Critical Commentary (T. & T. Clark)
NCBC	New Century Bible Commentary (Eerdmans)
NIBC	New International Biblical Commentary (Hendrickson)
NICNT	New International Commentary (Eerdmans)
NIGTC	New International Greek Testament (Eerdmans)
Pillar	Pillar Commentaries (Eerdmans)
Tyn	Tyndale New Testament Commentary (Eerdmans)
WBC	Word Biblical Commentary (Word)
WEC	Wycliffe Exegetical Commentary (Moody)

Matthew:

W. D. Davies, D. C. Allison (ICC)
D. Hagner (WBC)
D. A. Carson (EBC)

Mark:

R. Guelich (WBC)
C. E. B. Cranfield
W. L. Lane (NICNT)

Luke:

I. H. Marshall (NIGTC)

J. A. Fitzmyer (AB)
J. Nolland (WBC)
C. Evans (NIBC)

John:
G. R. Beasley-Murray (WBC)
R. A. Brown (AB)
R. Schnackenburg
D. A. Carson (Pillar)

Acts:
I. H. Marshall (Tyn)
F. F. Bruce (NICNT)
E. Haenchen

Romans:
J. D. G. Dunn (WBC)
C. E. B. Cranfield (ICC)
D. A. Moo (WEC/NICNT)
L. Morris (Pillar)

1 Corinthians:
G. D. Fee (NICNT)
H. Conzelmann (Herm)
C. K. Barrett (HNTC)

2 Corinthians:
V. P. Furnish (AB)
R. P. Martin (WBC)
C. K. Barrett (HNTC)

Galatians:
H. D. Betz (Herm)
E. D. Burton (ICC)
R. A. Longenecker (WBC)
F. F. Bruce (NIGTC)

Ephesians:
A. T. Lincoln (WBC)
M. Barth (AB)
F. F. Bruce (NICNT)

Philippians:
G. F. Hawthorne (WBC)
P. T. O'Brien (NIGTC)
M. Silva (WEC)

Colossians/Philemon:
    P. T. O'Brien (WBC)
    F. F. Bruce (NICNT)
    E. Lohse (Herm)
    N. T. Wright (Tyn)

1 and 2 Thessalonians:
    C. A. Wanamaker (NIGTC)
    E. Best (HNTC)
    I. H. Marshall (NCBC)
    F. F. Bruce (WBC)

1 and 2 Timothy, Titus:
    G. W. Knight (NIGTC)
    G. D. Fee (NIBC)
    J. N. D. Kelly (HNTC)
    M. Dibelius, H. Conzelmann (Herm)

Hebrews:
    W. L. Lane (WBC)
    H. Attridge (Herm)
    F. F. Bruce (NICNT)
    D. Hagner (NIBC)

James:
    P. H. Davids (NIGTC)
    S. Laws (HNTC)
    R. P. Martin (WBC)

1 Peter:
    P. H. Davids (NICNT)
    J. R. Michaels (WBC)
    J. N. D. Kelly (HNTC)
    E. G. Selwyn

2 Peter/Jude:
    R. J. Bauckham (WBC)
    J. N. D. Kelly (HNTC)
    E. M. B. Green (Tyn)
    R. Webb (NICNT)

1, 2, 3 John:
    R. A. Brown (AB)
    I. H. Marshall (NICNT)
    S. S. Smalley (WBC)

Revelation:
G. R. Beasley-Murray (NCBC)
R. H. Mounce (NICNT)
I. T. Beckwith
G. B. Caird (HNTC)

STEP 14.   Translation

A good translation not only renders the words of the original into their best English equivalents; it also reflects the style, the spirit, and even the impact of the original wherever possible. You are the best judge of what constitutes a faithful translation. Your familiarity with the passage in the original, and with the audience for whom you write or preach, allows you to choose your words to maximize the accuracy of the translation. Remember that accuracy does not require wooden literalism. The words of different languages do not correspond to one another on a one-for-one basis. Your translation should leave the same impression with you when you read it as does the original. A translation that meets this criterion can be considered faithful to the original.

Two books on Bible translation are very valuable. Both should be read in their entirety, rather than referred to only for specific information.

John Beekman and John Callow, *Translating the Word of God* (Grand Rapids: Zondervan Publishing House, 1974).

This book contains serious, thoughtful discussions of the special problems presented by translating Scripture from one language to another. There is advice on how to handle metaphors, similes, words with multiple meanings, idioms, etc.

Sakae Kubo and Walter Specht, *So Many Versions?* (Grand Rapids: Zondervan Publishing House, 1975; rev., enl. ed., 1990).

The authors review at length the major twentieth-century English translations of the Bible, providing copious examples from each, and commenting throughout on the translation techniques and assumptions involved.

For articles of all kinds on the theory and practice of translation, you should be aware of:

The Bible Translator (London, 1950–) [JAF 35]

Step 15. Application

Books on hermeneutics as application are more difficult to suggest, partly because one's interests here will depend significantly on one's confessional stance. Perhaps the best comprehensive study of the whole hermeneutical task is:

A. Berkeley Mickelsen, *Interpreting the Bible: A Book of Basic Principles for Understanding the Scriptures* (Grand Rapids: Wm. B. Eerdmans Publishing Co., 1963).

You should also know about three books that deal with interpreting the NT, including discussions of the various methodologies outlined in this book as well as sections on "application." Each also reflects a different confessional stance:

William G. Doty, *Contemporary New Testament Interpretation* (Englewood Cliffs, N.J.: Prentice-Hall, 1972).

Daniel J. Harrington, S.J., *Interpreting the New Testament: A Practical Guide;* New Testament Message, 1 (Wilmington, Del.: Michael Glazier, 1979).

I. Howard Marshall (ed.), *New Testament Interpretation: Essays on Principles and Methods* (Grand Rapids: Wm. B. Eerdmans Publishing Co., 1977). [JAF 515]

Another helpful book, dealing with the history of biblical interpretation, is:

Robert M. Grant and David Tracy, *A Short History of the Interpretation of the Bible;* 2d, rev. and enl. ed. (Philadelphia: Fortress Press, 1984).

An important book that brings the whole discussion up to date is:

Anthony C. Thiselton, *The Two Horizons: New Testament Hermeneutics and Philosophical Description with Special Reference to Heidegger, Bultmann, Gadamer, and Wittgenstein* (Grand Rapids: Wm. B. Eerdmans Publishing Co., 1980).

Another book that wrestles with the hermeneutical issues raised by the various genres of the Bible is:

Gordon D. Fee and Douglas Stuart, *How to Read the Bible for All Its Worth;* 2d ed. (Grand Rapids: Zondervan Publishing House, 1993).

Finally, probably the best single introduction to the methodology of expository preaching, with step-by-step guidance for actual sermon preparation, is:

James W. Cox, *A Guide to Biblical Preaching* (Nashville: Abingdon Press, 1976).

And the most useful book on preaching from the various genres of biblical literature, as well as a book full of helpful discussions on preaching itself, is:

Sidney Greidanus, *The Modern Preacher and the Ancient Text* (Grand Rapids: Wm. B. Eerdmans Publishing Co., 1988).

INDEX OF AUTHORS

Index of Scripture Passages